**FIRESIDE**

# 21 DAYS
## TO A
# TRAINED
# DOG

By

## Dick Maller

with

Jeffrey Feinman

■

*Illustrated by Wendy Frost*

A FIRESIDE BOOK
PUBLISHED BY SIMON & SCHUSTER
NEW YORK  LONDON  TORONTO  SYDNEY

Copyright © 1977 by Ventura Associates
All rights reserved
including the right of reproduction
in whole or in part in any form
A Fireside Book
Published by Simon & Schuster, Inc.
Rockefeller Center
1230 Avenue of the Americas
New York, New York 10020


FIRESIDE and colophon are registered trademarks
of Simon & Schuster, Inc.


Designed by Beri Greenwald
Manufactured in the United States of America

37  39  40  38                        pbk.


Library of Congress Cataloging in Publication Data


Maller, Dick.
21 days to a trained dog.

(A Fireside book)
Includes index.
1. Dogs—Training.  I. Feinman, Jeffrey,
joint author.  II. Title.
[SF431.M4  1979]    636.7'08'3    79-13866
ISBN 0-671-22504-9
ISBN 0-671-25193-7 Pbk.

To Mom, Laura, Sheryl, Robert, Michael . . .
and to Brandt, whose love and work were
the inspiration for it all

# CONTENTS

# 1
# THE
# 21-DAY BASIC
# OBEDIENCE
# COURSE

*The single most frequently asked question* about dog training is "When can I start training him?" There's no dog too old to learn, for one answer, but that isn't what the question usually means. What people are asking is "How young can I start training him?"

There's no set answer to when a puppy can profitably begin obedience training. Certainly no dog is too young to learn things. Puppies start to learn about the world the moment they leave their mothers' wombs. But most trainers agree that the attention span of a young pup is just too short to allow for rigorous training sessions. Mostly, the results of very early obedience lessons of the classic type are frustration for both owner and dog. You can't figure out why nothing is getting across to him, and he can't figure out, can't even remember from one minute to the next, what it is you want him to do. The best advice is to hold off on formal training sessions until the puppy is from four to six months old. By that time, some of the newness of it all will have worn off, and the dog will be ready to concentrate just a wee bit on what you're telling him.

Of course, you're training the dog in basic household manners long before six months, and you're training him in lots of other things, too. You're showing him just what to expect from his association with you and with other human beings. You're teaching him the exact meaning of lots of words and phrases that will later be used as commands. And you're training yourself to be aware of who this pet of yours really is. By the time you're ready to begin formal obedience training, you should be well aware of what this dog likes—what constitutes a genuine reward for him. Would he rather have his ears scratched with your knuckles than gnaw on a big knucklebone? Wonderful! Now you know just what to do to reward and praise him in training. And you'll be able to keep the butcher's bills down a bit, too.

In short, your dog's puppyhood is a time of the two of you getting to know each other. He's also getting to know the whole wide world at the same time, so it's clear why people who start advanced lessons early are usually disappointed. Like all other animals, immature dogs have certain periods when they are most open to new knowledge. Early development proceeds in such a way that puppies are more responsive to human handling when they're three weeks old than when they're two months. This is why home-raised puppies make much better pets than those raised in cages at the pet shop, or all alone with the mother out in the barn. It's simply that if puppies are handled early by people, they associate such handling with pleasure. If it never comes until they're much older, it's associated with threat.

Years and years and years of training experience have taught us that the period of openness to real obedience training never begins before the pup is four months old. Seeing Eye dogs aren't accepted for training until they're fourteen months old, and many trainers of circus dogs refuse to even look at a pooch until he passes his second birthday. So don't feel that the one-quarter-year mark is the moment of truth. It may be that a dog whose training starts at four months and a dog whose training is postponed until one year will both know exactly as much at eighteen months. Nobody has ever tested this one to be sure, but early learning may be much more for the sake of the master than for that of the dog. In any case, if it's very rapid progress you're after, wait until the dog is about two. But if you have the patience to work with the younger dog's shorter concentration, you'll find him a slower but willing pupil at about four to six months. When you start depends on what you hope to accomplish, how fast, and why.

Whatever your dog's disposition, you can be sure he loves praise. The only exception is the dog who isn't really on good terms with his master. But if you and your pet have established a normal relationship during his puppyhood, he has probably learned to value your approval over everything else, including snacks and tidbits. If you really pay attention, you'll soon discover exactly in what form Pluto likes his praise. Some dogs would rather be tickled; others want to be pounded on the back. Still others, the verbal types, would rather hear the approval than feel it. Whatever form it takes, positive reinforcement should always come in the form of praise or affection. A well-fed family dog has little need and even less desire for dog biscuits and bits of meat to encourage him to perform. And artificially starving your pet will only spoil his concentration and make him uncomfortable during every training session.

As for negative reinforcement, it's advisable only in cases in which you can convince the dog that the bad consequences came from the environment, not from you. The effects of old-fashioned punishment on any animal are to make him hate and fear you. True, he may perform in order to escape punishment, but only when you're around or when he thinks somebody else might come down on him. If he thinks that bad consequences are in the nature of the world —like getting wet when you go out in the rain—he will avoid the behavior that causes the uncomfortable feelings. If he thinks bad consequences come from you, he'll devise ways to avoid or sneak around you.

One of the best ways to distract a dog from undesirable behavior without getting him mad at you is to call him, then praise him for coming. Any command or sharp noise will turn him away from what he's doing momentarily. Call out, "Stop, Nestor!" When he looks up, call him over, and give him a pat for obeying you. Instead of making him resentful by punishing him, you'll make him more likely to come or stop, or whatever you want, the next time. Naturally, you'll have to use negative reinforcement sometimes, but tricks like this one will help keep it to a minimum.

Besides the emphasis on positive reinforcement, our training technique stresses *operant conditioning.* What this means to you is that to be effective, a trainer must wait until the behavior he wants to reinforce occurs *naturally.* Because this technique follows the natural behavior patterns of your pet, it requires perhaps a bit more patience in the beginning than other training methods. And it's quite true that you can teach Buster to "Sit" by just pushing down on his rear over and over while you repeat the command. Eventually he'll learn to associate the one thing with the other, and you'll have the feeling of having showed him how to do something he couldn't otherwise have figured out. What may surprise you is that this method actually takes longer than ours, and is less effective. An animal is really quicker and more willing to associate something he does all by himself—and gets praise for—with a command than he is to associate what you want from him with force. If you force him into a sitting position, he'll sit, all right, but he'll feel coerced, pushed around. If you just wait until he sits of his own accord—and he will eventually—you can accomplish more with a few words of praise than with ten dog-training classes.

The truth about those famous classes is that they train more owners than dogs. There's nothing wrong with that, of course. Lots of new dog owners don't know the first thing about dogs and their needs. A little training, or even a lot of training, can't hurt. But traditional training classes aren't the best way to build a working dog–master team. They make use of artificial military-type situations that have little or no resemblance to the dog's home environment. They offer the twin distractions of lots of people and lots of dogs to take your mind (and your dog's) off your work. And they substitute rote drill for the natural learning situation in which every other kind of learning takes place, for human and animal alike. It's no wonder that dogs trained this way are at their best in dog-show obedience trials and other formal occasions. These are the situations that most closely approximate the conditions under which the dogs learned obedience.

If you have ambitions for entering your dog in obedience trials, it might be a good idea to get him used to the hustle and hurry by taking him to a few old-style dog-training classes. But most of your training should be done on a one-to-one basis. Just you and the dog, and plenty of time to wait for the behavior you want to occur spontaneously. If you don't want to compete, there's no reason whatever for you to subject yourself or Wolf to any classes. If you want to engage in group activities, a cocktail party or a soccer game might be more to the point.

Here are some basic rules, distilled from years of working with dogs, to help you on your way to the well-trained pet. In fact, though the object is for the dog to be trained, these rules aren't about the dog. They're about you. If you conduct yourself properly, the dog will behave naturally and do just what you want. Though trainers sometimes speak of the limitations of the animal, the master really has to worry only about his own limitations. Your dog has, for example, infinitely more patience than you do. His whole life, after all, consists in learning how to get along with you and derive pleasure from your company. You are probably impatient to finish up with Ol' Spot and get back to *The Wall Street Journal*. A training session hardly ever has to be stopped because a dog loses his temper. The same cannot be said of trainers. Your dog will be more consistent than you are, and more attentive. The notion that dogs have short attention spans probably derives more from the impatience of owners than from any real failing on the part of the canines. These rules, in short, are to allow not for your dog's faults, but for yours.

1. Consistency pays. In training, always use the same words for the same ideas. For example, if you want to teach "down," don't say, "Lie down, Prince" one time and "Down, boy" the next. Keep the commands short, but most of all, make them the same, exactly the same, every time. If you use hand signals, the same goes for them.

2. Introduce commands slowly, and only after the dog has performed the behavior you want spontaneously. You wait. He sits. You say, "Good boy, Nugget. Sit. Good dog." In this way, the dog learns to associate word with action with pleasure—the only real winning combination in training anybody to do anything.

3. Make training sessions pleasurable for both of you. Play with the dog a few minutes before you start any kind of work, even just watching for the action you want to train. This doesn't mean you shouldn't be serious about training. You should. But be pleasant, friendly. The only taboo is laughing at the dog during training. You'll either humiliate him or turn him into a clown.

4. Keep sessions short, especially at first. Start with ten-minute sessions; work up to twenty. This is for your sake, really, so that you won't lose your temper and spoil all the effort the two of you have put in.

5. Patience, patience, patience. Not that the dog is such a slow learner. Far from it. But people often are unreasonable in their expectations. If your attitude is "Let's see what happens today," rather than "By gum, today he'll learn how to sit," you'll have better and faster results. If you manage to be relaxed and patient, you'll be rewarded

in the short run by a pleasanter session and in the long run by a better-trained dog.

6. End the session *before* the two of you tire of it. If you feel yourself getting short-tempered, stop there, even if you've been at it only five minutes.

7. Use praise as a reward, not food. Jock will perform for food only if he's purposely starved, which will hardly make him look forward to the sessions. Dogs will do for love what they would never consider for just a bite to eat.

8. Be firm. Both with the dog and yourself. If you pay attention to what you're doing, praising and rewarding the exact behavior you want, the dog will learn easily and correctly after a few times. If you are inattentive or lax, you'll only confuse poor Marigold and make your job lots harder. Be sure you see exactly what you want before you give reinforcement. Between sessions, reward the behavior whenever you see it. But don't be fanatical. If an animal is led to expect praise every single time he performs, he'll be disappointed and confused on the inevitable occasion you miss. In giving rewards, most of the time actually works better than all of the time.

9. Never punish. What you must do is arrange for unpleasant consequences to befall the dog when he misbehaves. This is entirely different from punishment, and much better for the purpose of training.

10. Use the dog's own name as part of moving commands only. Say, "Lucy, Come," or "Lucy, Heel." There's no sound so winsome as the sound of one's own name. (Do not use the dog's name for stationary commands such as "Down," "Sit" and "Stand.")

11. When you first start training, do it in the same place every day, and make sure there aren't any distractions. This is one reason why a training class isn't the ideal

place for real training, especially for beginners. After the pup has learned his lessons, you can work him in other surroundings so that he'll get used to performing under all conditions. At first, though, keep him isolated.

12. Never grab at the dog or run after him. At first, use only coaxing and praise. Later, work the dog on a leash with a training collar for control. If you chase or hit at him, you can make a dog hand-shy and almost impossible to handle.

13. Vary your tones with the appropriate words. Praise, of course, is given in warm, friendly tones. It doesn't matter a bit what you say, as long as it's the same every time, and as long as it's loving and warm. When a dog is new to an exercise, cajole him, coax him along. Later, when he can be expected to understand, use the commanding tone of voice. This last voice means you expect obedience, you demand it. Your dog is better than you are at recognizing shifts in tone, so be aware not of just what you say, but of how you say it. Avoid the irritable, crabby voice that sounds like whining. When that note starts creeping in, it's time to quit.

14. Be sure your pet is in the same happy mental state when you end the lesson as when you start. The simplest way to do this is to be sure *your* frame of mind is good. If you're still "up" and full of enthusiasm, the dog will be too.

15. Remember that commanding, and the sharp corrections that go with it, come only after the dog has learned to associate certain behaviors with praise and reward. In the beginning, you must wait for events to occur at random, then reward the ones you want to encourage. Don't bother to discourage behavior you don't want, unless it's extremely destructive, like biting.

# Basic Equipment

For ordinary obedience training, you need very few articles of equipment. Basically, you'll need a leash, a training or choke collar, and a long line. Even these are optional, and should not be used at the beginning when you're seeking out the behaviors you want to reward. You'll also need a spacious place to work your dog, one that is reliably people- and dog-free at the same hour every day. Later on, if you want your pet to learn to jump hurdles or to fetch and carry, for example, you'll need more equipment. But for the 21-Day Basic Obedience Course, the leashes and collar are ample. Firmly implant the leash concept in the dog's consciousness. If your dog is a city pet, accustomed to taking all his walks on the leash, it's a good idea to train him on the leash from the start. You can use the training collar too, mostly to get him used to wearing it. This collar isn't really intended to "choke" the dog at all; it's used to allow you greater control than you would have with a leash and regular collar. In fact, you'd be more likely to really choke the dog with a leather collar than with a chain. If the dog is used to running free, use work on the leash only to put the finishing touches on a routine he has already learned. Make the training sessions a continuation of the daily routine, as pleasant to him as all his other outings with you. That way, Morty will come to look forward to these sessions as favorite times when you pay him a lot of attention.

A word about the chain collar. The leash, as you hold it, should be fastened to the end of the collar that passes around the dog's neck on the side nearest you. The tightening and loosening of the collar is much easier to control when the collar is attached to the leash this way. If you are

right-handed, hold the leash in your right hand during training, teaching the dog to walk on your left. This leaves your
left hand, next to the dog, available for patting and encourag-
ing him. During ordinary walks, hold the leash in your left
hand, leaving the more frequently used right hand free for
other purposes.

Our formal exercises, while concurrent with the daily life
of the dog, are really very intensive training sessions. The
21-Day Basic Obedience Course is designed to concentrate
on just a few exercises, one every few days. But intense as
they are, the exercise sessions should not seem arduous to
either you or the dog. This is because the method is so natural, so easygoing, that neither of you may notice at first how
much is being accomplished.

# Days 1, 2, 3: Sit

We usually start with either the sit or the heel, depending
on whether or not a dog is used to walking on the leash. For
those who aren't, the sit is a good introduction to leash work.
For those who walk on the leash every day, it may be easier
to start with the heel. This is especially true if the dog has
been taught good leash manners already. If not, this is the
time to teach them.

The first time you and your dog go out for a formal training session, you must let him have his head. If he's on the
leash, fine, but let him go where he wants to. We have found
that the best places for training, particularly at first, are large
empty spaces such as deserted school playgrounds, open
fields, or public parks. The dog should have the impression
that you're there to amuse yourselves, that it's all very relaxed and easy. In fact, though the purposes are more than
just amusement, it should be a relaxing time, from start to
finish. You've decided in advance what behavior you want

*Praise when dog sits by himself.*

to train, and your only job, at first, is to wait until it happens.

The minute it does, training begins. Your dog sits. Excellent. You pet him, praise him elaborately. Don't give him the rush, though. Keep everything low-key. The second time, you should slip the word "Sit" in among the "Good boys" and "Good dogs." "That's it, Poppy," you say; "good dog. Sit. Very good. Yes, Poppy, Sit." He'll be delighted at the praise, won't even bother to wonder what it's for. But the lesson will have begun to sink in, painlessly. Keep up the training session for as long as you feel comfortable and at ease. As long as you don't try to force any behavior, but just reward the behavior you want, even an hour of training will be no strain on the dog. As always, when you feel yourself getting cross and impatient, quit.

Although we strongly recommend formal training sessions every day, you can't stop there. The need for a regular time and place to train is more yours than it is Rover's. He doesn't stop learning just because the lesson hour is over. But you might forget that your intention is to train him well and regularly unless you adhere to a schedule. Whatever you do with your dog, you will train him. The question is, will you train him consciously and thoughtfully to do as you wish, or will you train him in a haphazard manner? If you aren't careful, you'll inculcate bad habits that will later be very hard to break. Therefore, use the daily training session, but don't stop there. Once you've begun to teach Muffin to sit, watch for the behavior, and praise it. We repeat, it isn't necessary or even desirable to praise her every time she sits. Just most times. You can train, in this sense, at any time, in any place. Whenever you happen to see her sit in the proper manner, go over to her and give her a pat on the head. Don't forget to say the word "Sit," so that she'll get used to the association.

About time limits: Our training method is so relaxed and

easygoing, assuming that *you're* relaxed and easygoing, that there's no reason not to "train" up to an hour at a time. Remember, you're just wandering around with the dog, waiting for the action you want to train to happen naturally. During the 21-Day Basic Obedience Course, an hour in the morning and another in the evening would be fine, provided you're relaxed about it. If you follow this routine, and also "train" during other times when you think of it, the dog should certainly understand the concept of "Sit" within 3 days. Of course, the behavior will need more reinforcement than that. You'll have to continue to give your pet plenty of practice and plenty of rewarding praise for sitting. But he will know what's expected at the end of the 3-day period. He will have received the basic information. Any learning will die out if it isn't constantly practiced. The 21-Day program is for introducing obedience concepts to the dog. It's up to you to see that he performs every day. After all, that's why you're training him—so that he will be civilized and pleasant to live with every day.

Notice that our method of teaching your dog to sit doesn't necessarily involve any leash work, nor does it operate by having you push down on the dog's rump, jerk the training collar, or apply any such forceful treatment. Walk him as you usually do—not letting yourself be dragged around, but also not dragging the dog after you. Remember that you're trying to create a relaxed feeling. This is the only atmosphere in which the dog is likely to sit of his own accord. Most pet owners have no real need or desire for a militaristically trained animal who snaps to attention at the jingle of a leash. They just want a well-behaved canine member of the family; an animal whose behavior is reliable and friendly, and who won't make enemies among friends and neighbors. If this is what you had in mind for your dog, we believe our training method to be the most effective and efficient ever devised.

*The perfect sit.*

Just how perfectly your dog learns to sit depends on how refined your own demands are. If you're after the perfect sitting position, you must withhold your praise after a while except when the dog sits perfectly. A perfect sit is one in which the dog sits firmly on both hipbones, leaning neither left nor right. If you have the patience, you can train the dog to sit like this every time. At first, praise him for anything approximating a good sit. But after he's learned what the word means, be more demanding. Not that you need ever scold. Just hold back on your praise until you see the dog sitting as you wish. He'll quickly learn that "Sit" doesn't mean just putting his rump on the ground; that it means a very particular posture. One caution: if you really don't care how the dog sits, just so he's down, don't bother with the niceties. Training is for your convenience, and unless you plan to enter the dog in obedience trials, nobody but you will ever care whether the animal does an A sit or just a B-plus.

# Days 4, 5, 6: Heel

Dogs are taught to heel so that walking with them will be a pleasure instead of a footrace. Untrained dogs either run out ahead of you, pulling you along by the leash, or else hang back, forcing you to tug on them. How often have you seen a harried dog owner, out for the last walk of the evening at eleven o'clock, pulling poor Phoebe down the sidewalk by her neck, swearing under his breath? How much easier and more pleasant for both of them if Phoebe had been taught to walk along by his side, matching her pace to his. Strangely enough, heeling is often neglected in simple obedience training. Most dogs learn to sit, one way or another, and to lie down, and to come when called. But few people see the value of heeling, thinking that it's a trick appropriate only to police dogs.

But the heel is really one of the basics of dog obedience. Far from being a specialized attainment, it is one of the essentials that help to make your dog into a true companion rather than a burden. The real trick in teaching the dog to heel is in teaching him to pay attention to you. He doesn't wander off to sniff at the flowers because he doesn't like you; he does it because his attention is distracted. If he learns to watch you, to notice how fast you're walking and where you're headed, he'll have more than half the lesson mastered. The other part is that he must stay near you when walking, no matter how many interesting things may turn up to compete for his attention.

It's best to train the dog to heel by using the leash and collar. That way, you can correct him when his attention wanders. Once again, we emphasize that you correct him in such

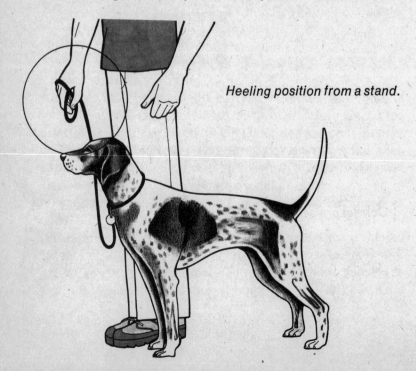

*Heeling position from a stand.*

*Quick tug.*

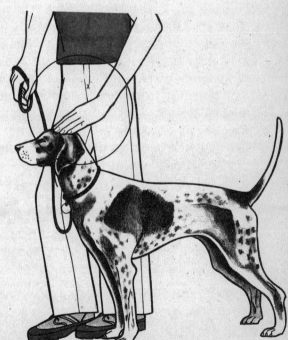

*Correct praise.*

a way that he thinks the correction a natural consequence of his actions, not a punishment initiated by you. Don't jerk the leash violently, so that Shep can see that you're doing the pulling. Instead, hold the leash in such a way that the dog is perfectly comfortable as long as he stays close to your left knee, but feels stress as soon as he moves away. Give plenty of praise whenever the dog keeps the leash slack by himself, but don't give him any slack yourself. As with the sit, you must wait until the dog is walking in the correct position, then reward him. Don't try to drag him into the heel position, though you can make it somewhat uncomfortable for him to strain on the line by just holding it firmly. Remember, when you're training the dog to heel on the left side, the leash should be held in your *right* hand. This gives you more control, and leaves your left hand free to pat him when he gets it right.

Remember that the point of this exercise is *not* for you to hold the dog at your side by force. The leash should be held slack when the dog is walking (or standing) in the right place. Whenever he lags behind or pulls ahead, give the leash a quick tug, then let it go slack again. Praise him when he returns to the correct position. But don't get into a fight with him. If you try to physically haul him into place, he'll resist, thinking it's either a game or a challenge to his honor. Either way, you'll be the loser. If he doesn't come into place on the first tug, give a series of sharp tugs until he reaches heel position. Don't look at the dog while you're giving these tugs, or in any way convey the impression that this is a contest of wills. Just wait until he finally does come alongside, then praise and reward him for doing right. If he experiences some discomfort when he's not at heel, you certainly aren't responsible for that. You're just pleased to see him walking so nicely, just as you wanted him to.

Once you've given your pet some practice in walking at

your heel (at your knee, really), you must start giving the command, so that he can associate word with deed. Always speak in a pleasant tone, saying, "Good boy, Ulster; that's right. Heel. Good dog." As often as you can, correct him by urging and coaxing him to come along, rather than by pulling on the leash. Save that for real reluctance, after training has progressed for several hours. The point of this and all our training is to give the dog the impression that somehow, just naturally, doing things one way is very comfortable and pleasant; doing them any other way mysteriously leads to less comfortable circumstances. This is very different from leading him to believe that he has to do things a certain way to escape your wrath. In the first instance, the animal has no resentment or hostility. It's just the way of the world, the same kind of thing as when he learned that you can't step off high places or you'll fall and get hurt. He doesn't blame anybody for that; it's just natural. Remember, too, that training to heel must begin with patient waiting on your part. You must wait for the dog to come to heel of his own accord, then praise him for it. Of course, you help by making it just a bit uncomfortable for him to walk anyplace else. But you don't give commands at first; and you don't battle him into submission, then or ever.

## Days 7, 8, 9: Turn

The turn follows naturally out of the training to heel. This is really just an extension of the heel training—coaching the dog to follow you and stay in his place no matter what you do. It's fine to have a dog who'll stay at heel as long as you stand still or walk in a straight line. But it's really useful only if the dog will walk at your heel no matter what sort of fancy maneuver you perform. Once you've taught your pet these

first three lessons—the sit, the heel, and the turn—he'll behave like the perfect companion when you take him walking.
For most pet owners, that's half the battle. Many people
never have any trouble they can identify with the dog as long
as he's at home. But taking him out for a walk can be a
painful ordeal. Either he's tugging at the leash, making you
feel like the front part of a dogsled, or he's hanging behind,
making you feel like a two-year-old with a pull toy. If you
let him off the leash, you might not see him again for an hour.
It is at this point that lots of owners begin to feel that they've
taken on a bit more than they can handle. They either turn
to some system of training—or give up the dog.

Before you reach that point, provided you haven't already, resolve to follow the 21-Day course through to its end.
If you do, you'll have transformed your dog from an unruly,
essentially wild animal into a civilized companion. As you
progress, you'll see how lessons blend one into another.
Turns, for example, should be done on a leash, just as training to heel was done. Command the dog to the heel
position, then walk with him. Remember to take small steps
if your dog is a dachshund or other short-legged breed. Once
he's trained, you can certainly expect him to walk with you
at your normal stride. But for the purposes of instruction, it's
better to try to match the length of your steps to his.

The important thing about teaching the dog to make turns
with you is that you must make the turn first, then correct the
dog for not watching. Correction, once again, does not mean
punishment. It means giving a short pull on the leash, sufficient to let the dog know that he's not in the heel position,
where he's supposed to be. You should do this when the
dog isn't looking, so that he'll blame himself for his inattention, not you for your harshness. As you pull the leash, say,
"Apricot, Heel." As soon as he returns to the heel position,
praise him elaborately. You must also remember to praise

him if he does it right in the first place. But if correction is necessary, do it with a jerk of the leash; then immediately give the command, and let the leash go slack again. To accomplish all this, you must make the turn yourself before you can correct the dog.

To make a right turn, pivot quickly on your right foot, immediately stepping away from the dog to catch him when he isn't looking. The left turn should be made on the left foot, right in front of the dog, so that you bump him with your knee. You must not do this vindictively or in any way give the impression that you're angry with the dog. You've just made a turn and he, through his inattention, has bumped into you. Unless you behave like a threatening monster, your dog will certainly assume that it's all his fault and snap back to the heel position. Just think of how apologetic he always is when you step on his foot by accident around the house. If he doesn't immediately resume the proper position, give one pull on the leash and the command "Moby, Heel."

Because teaching the dog to make turns at heel involves action, it's somewhat harder to apply our basic principle of waiting until the desired behavior appears spontaneously. But there will be times, more and more as the days go on, when the dog turns perfectly with you. Don't forget to be lavish with your praise at such times. The praise, as a reinforcement, has far more effect than the leash tugs and commands do. It is this positive reinforcement which really convinces the dog that he wants to do as you say. The corrections are just the way of communicating what is expected, and should be kept to a minimum. It is not necessary, in this or any other obedience exercise, to give candy or tidbits as rewards. Your approval is far more effective and better for the dog than food.

You should also practice making complete turns—that is, about-face—with the dog on the leash or at heel. You must

*Right turn.*

*Left turn.*

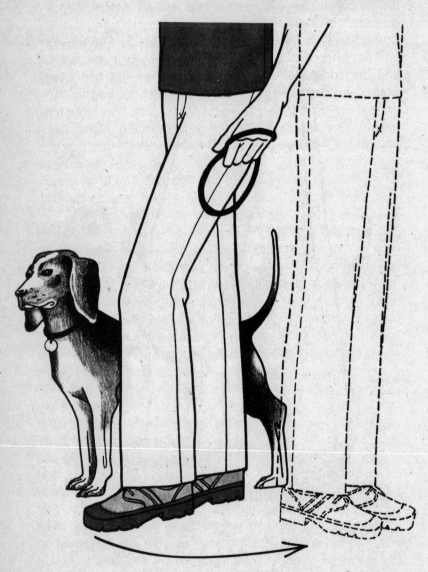

*About-face.*

turn rather quickly when practicing this, so that the dog will be caught looking away and have to scramble to catch up. Corrections are made in the same manner as with the right and left turns: just a quick pull on the leash if you need it, and the command to "Heel." As soon as the dog obeys, praise and pat him for his good behavior. Of course, if he makes the turn successfully without correction, you must also make a fuss over him. If you make a very quick about-face to the left, you'll have to pass the leash from hand to hand in back of you. This may take a little practicing on your part before you start working with the dog. The other way to take a left about-turn is to walk all the way around the dog. Then he must walk around too, in order to stay at heel.

While you're practicing the heel and the turns, take some care to vary your speed of walking. The dog should get used to keeping up with you no matter whether you're in a hurry or out for an easy stroll. You, after all, are the boss, and the pace of your walk is determined not by how long your hound's legs are, but by how fast you want to go. Walk with the dog in heel position, and praise him when he does it right. Make quick changes from one pace to another, always giving rewards to your dog when he maintains his spot at your left knee. Try making sudden stops, to see if he'll stop with you. When he does, tell him he's a good dog, and give the command to sit. If you always remember to combine what he knows in this way, you'll soon have a dog who will automatically sit whenever you come to a stop. This will no doubt make him the best-behaved animal for miles around, and people will start to think you've taken old Red to some fancy school. An extra dividend from this good behavior is that your praise will become warmer and more genuine once you start to see a few results from all your effort. And when the praise is richer, it will be even more effective in acting

*Make turn around dog;*
*he will have to stand "at heel."*

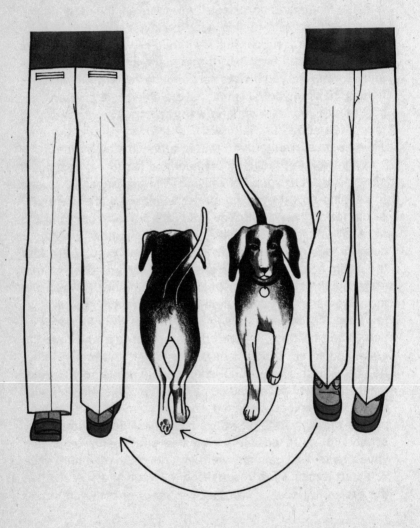

*Teach dog to pass
on the correct side of posts.*

6 feet

as a reward and a reinforcement to your dog. That's why training progresses with gathering speed as time goes by. And that's what makes it possible to accomplish so much in well under a month.

A good exercise to do with your dog when you feel he's pretty good on the turns is the figure-8. This involves the use of two objects to circle around: chairs, trees, even people, if they promise not to distract the dog. Place the two objects about six feet apart, and move around them in a figure-8. Correct the dog if he tries to pass on the wrong side of the object. This will get him used to staying in the heel position in crowded street situations and other places where people or objects might get in the way. It's also a good way for you to check his progress as a well-trained heeler.

## Days 10, 11, 12: Stand

Suppose you don't really want a dog who automatically sits whenever you stop? But you do want some command, don't you, to give him if there's going to be a delay, or if you just want him to stay where he is? The command is "Bobo, Stand." It can be taught on the leash, as can all the exercises in the program, but you have to remember in this one not to pull on the leash or try to use it for controlling the dog. Begin, as usual, by searching out the correct behavior and praising it. Stop during your walks with the dog, and if he stops and stands still, tell him, "Good boy, Andy, Stand." If he starts to sit down, try scratching his rump to make him stand up again, then heap on the praise when he does it .

At first, aim only at getting the dog to stand when you tell him to, rather than starting right out with the stand-stay. If he stands still a millisecond the first few times, that's enough

*Scratch back to make dog stand.*

for you to reward him with hugs of joy. As time goes by, however, you get a bit more demanding. If he breaks from the stand, you must gently lead him back to that position, tell him again to stand, then praise him if he does it. The back-scratching method is a good method of getting dogs to stand. If it doesn't work on your particular pet, find out what does, and use it. We feel that it is a bad idea to force dogs to stand by such methods as holding them up or dragging them up by the leash. But you will find that keeping the dog in a standing position is a lot easier than getting him back up again once he has sat or even lain down.

If you want to teach a dog hand signals for this or any other exercise, you must use them faithfully throughout the training. The traditional signal for the stand-stay is to drop your left hand to your side and hold it there, palm facing backward. It is the easiest thing in the world to teach a dog to respond to hand signals, provided you *always* use the signals when first training a dog in an exercise. If you do this without fail, you'll find it a simple matter to go back later and exercise the dog without speaking a single command. Some owners don't want to be bothered with hand signals, but others find them incomparably useful in situations where they don't want to be barking commands. If you plan to hunt with your dog, or just take him to a lot of crowded public places, hand signals might be just what you need.

The stand exercise extends naturally into the stand-stay. You don't need a separate command for this one, since the dog is supposed to catch on that "Stand" means to stand until he's told differently. You have to gradually extend the time you require your dog to stand. Test him by stepping away from him. At first, just back off, watching him all the while, and giving the hand signal, if you use it. If the dog starts to break from his stand, or to sit down, try taking a

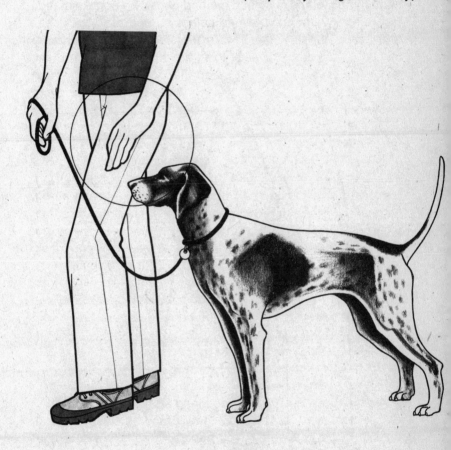

*Stand-stay hand signal
(Step away on right foot only).*

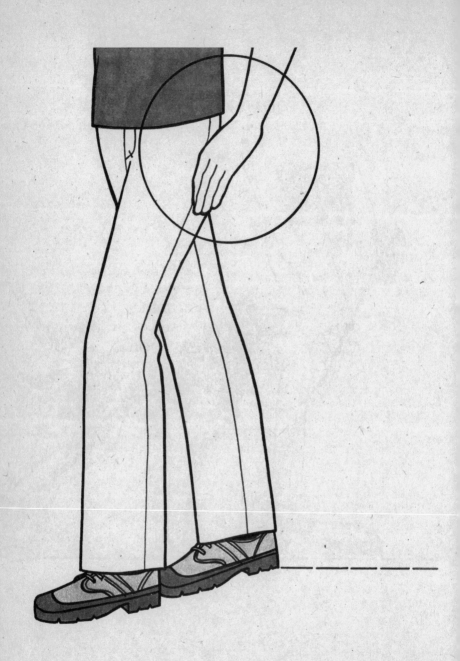

*Stand-stay*
*(Step away on right foot only).*

quick step toward him. This will probably bring him up short, and give you a chance to praise him again. In our method of training, we aim to increase the number and frequency of right things the dog does. Any means you can devise to get the dog into the position you want will allow you another chance to praise him. And the more praise he gets, the quicker he'll learn the trick. Keep walking toward him, if necessary, in order to make him hold his position. Eventually, when he's really steady, you should be able to walk all around him without causing him to leave the standing position. The first time this happens, you'll probably be ecstatic. But don't give in to the temptation to rush the dog and give him a big hug. This will certainly make him leap out of position, and will defeat what you're trying to accomplish with the use of positive reinforcement. Be generous with praise, of course, but never get yourself or the dog overexcited.

## Days 13, 14, 15: Sit-Stay

It's usually better to teach the sit-stay after the stand, since the notion has already been introduced that you expect the dog to stay where you put him. Having learned this idea gradually in the course of the stand exercises, he'll readily understand what you mean when you tell him to sit and stay. At this point, if you haven't already, you'll have to introduce the command "Stay." Since Poochie knows how to sit, just tell him to sit-stay. Move away from him, and praise him when he stays seated. Be careful not to be too effusive in your praise, or he'll leap up to be at your side. Just speak soothingly, telling him he's a good dog and repeating the command to sit and stay. The gentlest way to correct a dog who refuses to remain in place is to move him back—picking him up if he's small, leading him on the leash if he's big. Put him back where you want him to sit, then reward him with praise if he stays there. If you want to, you can teach the sit-stay on the leash. For this one, it's better to use the long line mentioned as training equipment. This allows you to move quite a distance away from the animal, still maintaining contact via the leash. If the dog starts to inch toward you as you move away, try flipping the leash sharply so that it nicks him under the chin. Once again, this has to be done in such a way that he doesn't blame you for punishing him. Never call out, "No!" as you do this, or do anything else to give the impression that you're angry.

Once the dog is a bit steady on the sit-stay, test him by walking around him, just as you did with the stand. If he breaks while you're in back of him, or across the yard, go over to him and put him back in place. The worst thing you can do is to start yelling at him from several yards away, to rush him menacingly, or in any other way to threaten him. For this reason, you can't correct him from a distance. Retain your composure, go back to where your dog is, and lead him to the spot where you want him to sit. As in all exercises, you must give praise in graduated stages. At first, you reward the dog for any approximation of the correct behavior, no matter how brief. If he stays for one second, you tell him he's a good boy. But after a while, he has to stay for a significant length of time before he wins your approval. Since the ultimate object of the sit-stay training is to make your dog stay until you tell him not to, you must always extend the time before he can win praise by just sitting. When he's perfectly trained, he'll get his reward when you call him to you, thereby breaking the sit.

As the dog gets better and better at the sit-stay, you test him in more and more demanding ways. Walk away from him until you are out of sight. Get a chair and a book and

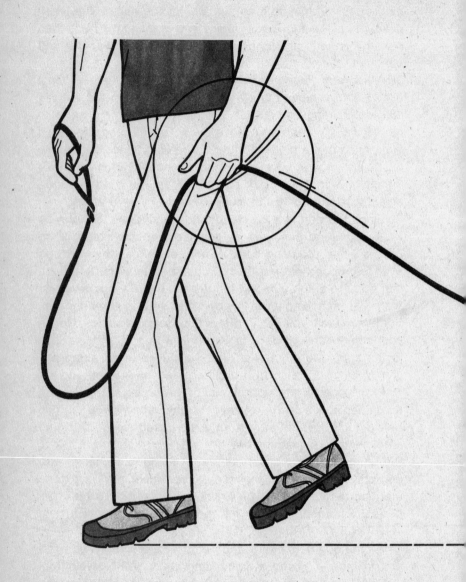

*Sit-stay. Snap lead straight up
and say "Sit, stay."*

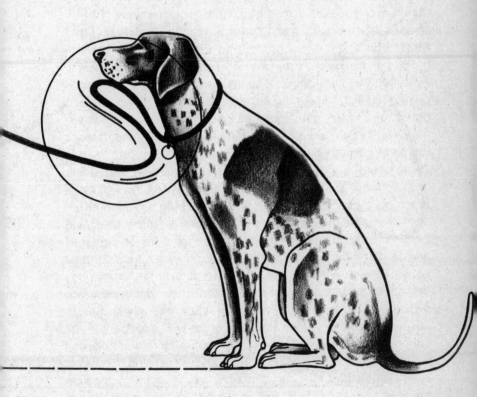

sit down behind him, pretending to read. At first, when he sees you actually ignoring him, the dog will undoubtedly break and come over to get your attention. But you don't let him get away with it. He must learn to stay whether or not you're watching. Take him back to his place and admonish him firmly to "Sit-Stay." A well-trained dog will sit for fifteen or twenty minutes while his owner is out of sight or otherwise engaged. You'll be able to teach him the basic concept in well under three days, but he needs constant work to reach the level of patience you want. Like all the exercises of basic obedience, the sit-stay should be practiced every day. Don't forget that a dog—or a person, for that matter—can be untrained if he never uses his lessons in everyday life. Do everything you can think of to increase the dog's steadiness on the sit-stay. Make noise, whistle, bang things, send a bunch of children chasing a ball past where the dog is sitting. He has to learn that absolutely nothing constitutes a legitimate excuse for breaking from the sit.

At about this point in the training period, you may begin to experience the plateau effect. In the first few days of training, it's all great fun for the dog. He's getting so much attention from you that this seems like the best time he's ever had. But after a while, he perceives that a lot of demands are being made on him, and boredom may set in. You must convince him with firm authority that this is the way things are going to be from now on and that if he wants your approval (which he does) he has to practice willingly and regularly. Or maybe you're the one who will experience the slump. The first thrill of progress is beginning to wear off, and the dog seems to be slowing down in his learning. You start to feel a distinct longing to play tennis in the evenings instead of training Junior. But this is exactly the crucial time. Be firm with yourself as well as your pet. Once you get past this sticking point, the pace will pick up again, and both of you will accept training as part of your daily lives. Remember that in any learning, there are periods of rapid progress followed by periods when nothing seems to be happening, at least to an outside observer. But these blank times are when the temporary new learning is being transferred to the permanent memory. Practice must be kept up during these apparently fallow times; otherwise there will be backward progress. If you realize that this is the normal way the mind works in assimilating new ideas, you'll have more patience with the dog through the slow stretches.

# Days 16, 17, 18: Lie-Down

Except possibly for the sit, the lie-down is the most important household command. If your dog is utterly reliable in this matter, you can take him anywhere. He'll be a welcome guest in even the most fastidious homes (barring allergy) if you can order him to curl up unobtrusively in some corner and count on him to stay there. If you use hand signals, you can command your dog to drop at a distance, even if he's too far away to hear you clearly. All in all, it is extremely useful to train this command carefully and thoroughly. The traditional hand signal for the lie-down is to raise your hand as if you were going to strike the dog. Don't worry about bad associations on the part of the dog. As long as you aren't in the habit of striking him, he'll learn only that you want him to lie down.

What's different about our way of teaching the lie-down is that we emphatically don't recommend that you push the dog into the down position, pull him down with the leash, or in any other way use force. The trick is to teach Fala what you want without pushing him to perform. Performance comes later, after you're sure he understands what's expected. The

*Traditional lie-down hand signal
(left hand down as you bring right up).*

method is the same as in all the other commands. You must wait until you see him doing what you want, then offer praise and encouragement. Of course, you are free to start encouragement long before you're ready to initiate formal training. Whenever you see him lying at ease, give him a pat on the head and say, "Good dog. Lie down. That's it; good boy." Soon he'll associate the words with the idea. After that has been accomplished, you can reasonably expect him to learn to obey the command when he hears it.

As to which command to use, there is some disagreement among trainers. Some people think that just plain "Down" carries more force, while others prefer "Lie down." Whatever word or phrase you use—and it can be in Urdu for all the difference it makes to the dog—use it with absolute consistency. If you do, it won't take your pet long to understand. After that, it's just a matter of practice. Make him lie down with gesture and command. If he gets up again before you've released him, give the command again. You may have to put him back in place sometimes, using the time-honored method of pulling his forelegs out in front of him and lowering him back down from the sitting position. If you like to use the long line, practice dropping him from a distance while he's attached to the line. If he fails to obey, just give a short tug on the lead to remind him where his duty lies. This isn't the same thing as pulling him down by force with the leash, which we discourage. Be sure that you keep one hand—always the same one—free to give the hand signal if you use it. Signals must be used with absolute consistency if you want the association among command, signal, and action to be complete.

Although it's basic to good obedience, the lie-down is often harder to teach than the sit, heel, or stand. This is probably because a dog feels very vulnerable in the lie-down position, and his instincts tell him not to stay that way for

*Manual method to teach
dog to sit.
Push rump down.*

long. If anything attracts his attention or interest, not to mention exciting or scaring him, every impulse tells him to get to his feet. Nevertheless, good training can overcome all these impulses and cause him to obey only you. Some dogs, however, fight hard before they learn to be reliably steady on the lie-down. Rather than forcing a reluctant animal to lie down by pulling or pushing him, you must redouble your efforts to reinforce his every positive action with lots and lots of praise. You may find it much slower going than the other exercises you've encountered so far. Or you might be pleasantly surprised to discover that your dog accepts this as just another requirement of living with you, no better and no worse than all the others.

Some trainers who are inclined to use positive reinforcement with most other commands recommend force with the lie-down. Since some dogs, particularly large ones, can be rather hostile about being commanded into what they consider an inferior or indefensible position, some handlers think that the only way to win is to cuff, switch, force, or otherwise coerce the animal. We do not subscribe to this notion. Quite the contrary. Since the dog feels particularly threatened by this command, you should go out of your way to make him feel that there is nothing more pleasant than obeying his master and winning his approval. Instead of beatings, you should provide much reassurance and encouragement to the dog who feels hostile or fearful about the lie-down.

## Days 19, 20, 21: Come

Also known to dog handlers as the recall, this is the final exercise in our 21-Day Basic Obedience Course. Most dog owners find that their dogs come pretty reliably without any training at all. After all, if the relationship between trainer and animal is a good one, the dog wants to be where you are. He's overjoyed to hear you call his name, and just as happy to be summoned to be with you. But the truly obedient dog comes when you want him to—every time. Ninety-percent obedience just isn't enough.

The reason that your dog is already fairly good on the recall is that you have undoubtedly used, without even noticing it, our method of positive reinforcement to encourage this trick. You've been doing it, just as we suggest, since the very first day Buster came into your house as a tiny puppy. By now, he feels, at least most of the time, that the very most pleasant place to be is at your side. He expects, and usually gets, pleasure from obeying the call to "Come." The trick now is to make the association so strong in his mind that he'll be utterly reliable. This isn't just for the sake of precision obedience, but for the dog's safety as well. If he's ready to drop everything and come when you call him, you can stop him from darting into the street, running into the path of a weapon, or any other dangerous situation he might not be able to handle alone.

To steady your dog on the come, it's a good idea to make use of the long line. Hook it up to the dog's collar, and call him from across the yard. If he doesn't respond immediately, give a sharp, brief tug on the line. You may have to do this more than once before he gets the idea that you want him not just to come, but to come right away. A well-trained dog responds snappily to your commands and comes at a brisk trot when he's called. Don't forget to lavish praise on him when he does come. You probably won't have to use the line very much at first, since the dog is used to obeying this command. But keep the exercise up and after a while he'll get a little bored. He may start to come to you, then be distracted by something in the yard. As soon as he shows any signs of inattention, give him a little pull with the leash to remind him of his duty. If you spend three days of short sessions this way, he'll get the idea that you really mean business. Exercises like this one—done on the lead and with some rigor—can't be pursued for an hour or even half an hour; ten to twenty minutes at a time is plenty, though you can schedule two such sessions a day if you think it's necessary.

Another trick is to throw something at the dog when he isn't looking. The idea isn't to hit or hurt him, but to startle him out of his reverie and make him remember what he's supposed to be doing. You can use the short and noisy length of chain left over from other exercises, or anything else that will have a surprising and slightly unpleasant effect. Be sure that the dog doesn't see you throwing the object, or he'll feel threatened. If you can, get the cooperation of one or two friends who will do the throwing; that way, you won't be the guilty party at all. Other people can be useful in another way. Station a few friends around the yard with instructions to rebuff your dog when he comes up to them. It's quite all right if these people threaten him mildly, since you want him to feel that the most pleasurable thing he can do is come to *you.* Call him, and if he feels like running away, he'll probably run up to one of your friends for protection. When he does, he'll be surprised to find that the person he chooses offers no protection whatever. It won't take him long to realize that doing what you ask—every time—is the best policy.

For the dog who isn't reliable on the recall at all, you'll have to use more coaxing and soft words. Train him on the long line, but keep it slack most of the time. When the dog hesitates, pat your leg, clap your hands, and cajole him with a soft tone. Another trick that often works with the reluctant dog is to turn and walk away from him when he won't

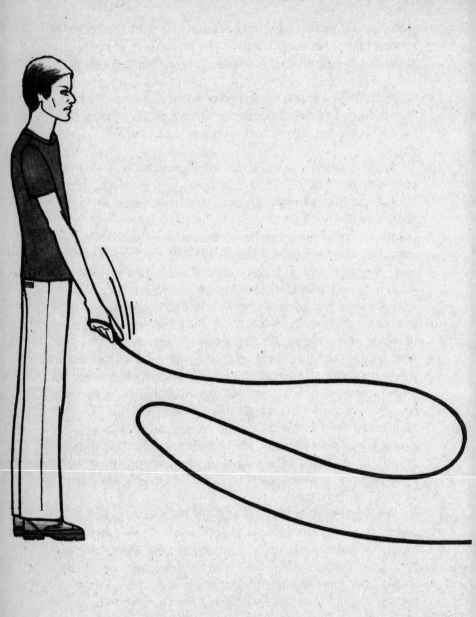

*Long yard line.*
*Call him to come right away;*
*sharp tug if he doesn't.*

*Throw chain behind him
to refresh his attention.*

come. He'll probably start trotting to catch up. When he does, turn and face him, and make him sit at your heel. Then praise him extravagantly—scratch his back, whatever he likes the most. Since he's slow to come to you in the first place, he may have bad associations that have to be broken through. Or maybe he just hasn't been made to feel that there's much pleasure to be expected from coming when called. In either case, you have to train him for a while to like coming to you. If your dog is in this latter category, you can profitably train him a bit longer than ten or twenty minutes. The rule is, if you're working on beginning exercises, the ones that involve a lot of praise and very little demand, you can keep it up a bit longer. As soon as either of you shows signs of irritability, it's time to stop. The dog, by the way, will seldom get impatient unless you do. Remember to test your dog on the recall at times other than the training period. Call him from across the yard when he's playing with the children, for example, or any time when he's busy with his own affairs. If he's well schooled, he should drop everything to come to his trainer. The only exception that comes to mind is just after the dog has been given a new bone. It's really too much to expect him to drop the bone to come, and he might suspect you of wanting to take it away from him. If he refuses to come at this time, don't fault him, as long as his other performances are good.

These seven exercises—the sit, heel, turn, stand, sit-stay, lie-down, and come—are the 21-Day Basic Obedience Course. When you have finished this program of training, your dog will know how to do these things. But remember, he'll know them the way a second-grader knows how to read. Without continued practice, he'll tend to forget his training. At the very least, he'll forget that he's expected to obey *every* time, whether he feels like it or not. It's a good idea

*Friend rebuffs dog when he comes to her.*

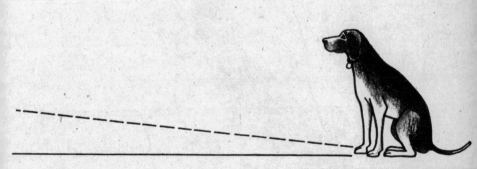

*Praise elaborately; scratch back and head.*

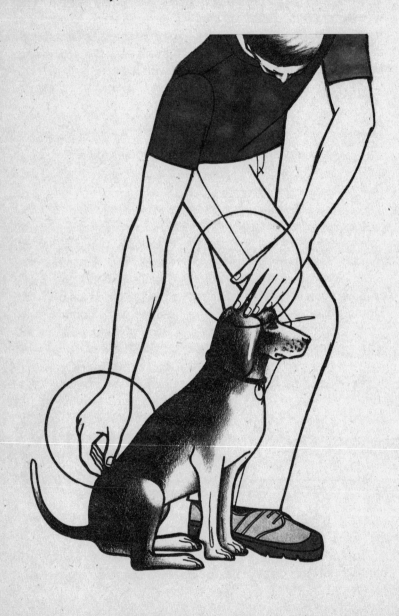

to work your dog for a few minutes every day, just as you would if you used him for hunting or farm work. Here are a few combination exercises you might want to use when putting your pet through his paces. This will vary the action and keep both of you from getting bored with it all.

# The Down-Sit

This is simply practice in going from the lie-down position to the sit and back again. If you have been training the dog to recognize hand signals, this one will be easy for both of you. The signal for the sit is to turn the palm of your hand upward, giving a slight upward motion, as if you were directing somebody to hang that picture just a little bit higher. Since he knows the command "Sit," he shouldn't have any trouble figuring out what you want, but the hand signals make it that much more graphic. When he's in the sitting position, drop him to the lie-down with command or signal or both. Keep this up until he responds quickly to your commands and stays in the desired position until you tell him to break it. You may want to use the leash for this exercise, just as a reminder. Don't forget to praise him every time he performs, at least in the beginning. After he seems to be obeying quickly and without reluctance, you don't have to reward him each and every time. If he comes to expect unfailing praise, he'll hold it against you on that inevitable occasion when you forget.

# The Sit-Down-Come-Heel

Obviously, this is a comprehensive review exercise, including all the really basic ideas of simple obedience.

*Signals for sit and down.*

Actually, we usually practice the skills in this order: Come-heel-sit-down-sit. But your well-trained dog should be able to act out any combination of the basic exercises. Don't work the dog too fast at first, and don't confuse him—and your-self—with commands like "Come" when you and he are in the same place. The object of the combined exercises isn't to attain lightning speed, but to get the dog used to obedi-ence in any combination of circumstances. You'll be very disappointed if your pet behaves perfectly in the training yard and runs away from you out on the street. For this reason, you should start to work him in strange places, in crowds, even in the car. He mustn't get the idea that obedi-ence is place-connected, or even person-connected. Let others in the family work the dog once in a while, so that he won't think you're the only one he has to obey.

If you follow the exercises outlined in this chapter, you will indeed produce a fully trained pet in only 21 days. To summarize, these are the major points you should keep in mind while training your dog:

1. Positive Reinforcement. Much more is done—by hu-mans and animals alike—to get something positive than to avoid something negative. It is well known that dogs will go through fire, quite literally, to help a master they love. Pain and punishment are poor teachers, and some of the lessons they teach are the ones no master wants his dog to learn. Punishment tells your dog to be afraid of you; not to trust you; to do what you wish out of in-timidation. Positive reinforcement teaches him that the most pleasurable thing to do is just what you tell him. Sometimes dog owners are deceived by what seem to be the instant results of punishment. One spanking seems to make a dog obey, while it takes many, many trials with praise and patting to show appreciable results. In fact,

*Come-heel-sit-down-sit.*

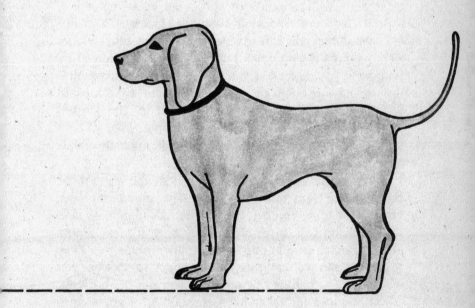

negative consequences do show quicker results, but the undesirable side effects are immediate too, and very long-lasting. Once a dog has been taught to be afraid of a person or people, it takes months or years to coax him out of it. Praise and love make for slower progress, but each step is in exactly the right direction, with no built-in conducement toward errors that have to be corrected later.

While we discourage trainers from the use of punishment, we do advise occasional correction. The difference, as you have seen, is that correction must be seen by the dog as coming from the neutral environment, rather than from an angry or hostile master. You do not punish your dog, but you arrange for unpleasant consequences to befall him. This notion virtually precludes hitting, since most dogs will be quick to figure out what happened, even if they weren't looking when the blow fell. But flinging something noisy in the dog's direction often works well, as does a very quick tug on the leash, followed by release. If you do it right, the dog will always blame himself for having been so foolish. He might even look to you for comfort. If he does, be sympathetic. This kind of training establishes trust between dog and owner while it enforces obedience. It is this combination which makes for great working teams.

2. Operant Conditioning. This means that you wait for the behavior you want, then reinforce it. This is different from, and better than, forcing the dog to do something and then praising him or rewarding him for it. It takes a little more patience on the part of the trainer, since you have to just sit and wait until the dog happens to do what you want. But you can do this any time you see the behavior —not just in a formal training session; so if you're in a rush, you can still train very quickly. Like negative rein-

forcement, forcing the desired behavior has unpleasant side effects that are difficult to get rid of. Most dogs feel some resentment when they are pushed into the sitting position, for example, or choked by the collar to keep them lying down. Dogs trained this way often think up unusual ways of defying their masters, or else they harbor a secret hostility that makes them unreliable as companions. Force works, especially if the dog is then rewarded, but patience works even better in the long run. If you wait for the dog to act, you give him the impression that he does what he does of his own free will. Training by operant conditioning produces a dog who obeys joyfully. He's under the impression—not entirely false—that he obeys because he *wants* to. Naturally, this makes him a more joyful and fulfilling companion.

3. Intermittency. This just means that you don't have to try to reinforce your dog *every* time he does what you want. Most of the time works better than every time. We humans shouldn't try to make our pets think we're infallible. They may be so disappointed when they find out we're not, they'll have a nervous breakdown. Or at any rate, a breakdown in training. Be steady and consistent, but not compulsive.

4. Patience. This isn't exactly a separate psychological principle, but it can hardly be overemphasized. Whenever you lose your temper, you're punishing the dog. And punishment works against you almost as much as it works for you. Remember that the dog is much more patient than you. If you don't get crabby, neither will he. Watch yourself for signs of irritability, and when you see them, stop training. You'll accomplish nothing in that mood anyway.

5. Forgiveness. This is mostly for yourself. Of course, perfect patience and nonviolence are the ideal. But no

one should expect himself or his dog to live up to the ideal all the time. If you do lose your temper and whack poor Buck, don't go into shock. Make it up to him with a little love, then go on as before. The only thing that leads to trouble is if you make it a principle to use punishment. Believe it or not, your dog understands that everybody has a bad day. Be ready to forgive yourself for a little irascibility. Be ready to forgive the dog, too, though dogs are invariably lots more patient than people.

# II
# ADVANCE OBEDIENCE

*Retrieving.*

*After you've completed* the 21-Day Basic Obedience Course, you might wish to go on training your dog. Perhaps you want to enter him in obedience competitions. He can earn Companion Dog, Companion Dog Excellent, and Utility Dog designations in competitions authorized by the American Kennel Club. Unfortunately, these trials are open only to purebred dogs, so your mutt will have to win his ribbons in unauthorized shows. But there are lots of those around too, if competing is your thing. Or maybe you have no interest in dog shows, but you've discovered you enjoy working with your pet and seeing him master new lessons. Either way, there are many tricks and functions he can learn beyond basic obedience. Any of these will make him a pleasure and a useful friend to you.

The main thing that distinguishes CDX (Companion Dog Excellent) dogs from CD (Companion Dog) dogs is that the former jump and retrieve. There are many exercises designed to accomplish the transition, and we offer a few of the most common and effective. If you're interested in AKC competitions, you should equip yourself with obstacles just like the ones your dog will encounter at obedience trials. This means that besides the equipment you already have for the 21-Day course, you'll need: a regulation dumbbell, a jumping stick or broomstick, a bar hurdle, a long hurdle, and a solid hurdle. If you're training purely for your own pleasure, you can improvise. The dumbbell, of course, is to teach the dog to retrieve. The stick and the hurdles are for various kinds of jumps, and you can probably devise good substitutes if you're not out to win prizes. We do recommend that you buy a regulation dumbbell, just because it's a very easy thing for the dog to carry in his mouth. A rolled-up newspaper is just about the best homemade substitute we've found.

# Drop on Recall

The first advanced lesson is just a continuation of basic training, but it's an exercise that's particularly hard. It's hard because what you're asking of the dog is that he stop in his tracks and lie down even though he's been called to come to you. Even the most obedient and good-natured dogs have a bit of trouble believing this one at first. After all, they seem to say, you've called me. Don't you want me to come? But if Rags has learned his early lessons well, he'll soon catch on that you expect obedience, whether or not he understands the reason. Like the recall itself, the drop on recall is a lifesaver. If you can imagine your dog running to greet you across the path of a car, then you can imagine how this trick could be used to save his life.

The exercise is just a combination of the come with the lie-down. Call the dog to you, but then give him the command to lie down. You should give the second command before the dog gets up a lot of speed; otherwise you're asking something that's almost physically impossible. At first, the dog will look at you as if you've taken leave of your senses. Insist, however, and he'll resign himself to just one more bit of incomprehensible human whimsy. Most dogs stop when you give the command to lie down, but then they just stand there. To show that you really mean it, go over to the dog and give the command again, reinforcing it with the hand signal, if you use it. If he ignores the lie-down command altogether, toss the wadded-up leash or a clod of earth at him to startle him. He'll stop then, and you'll give the lie-down command once again. If, by some chance, the dog drops on the first trial, wait a minute, call him to you, and praise him at length. Don't offer too much praise to him when he just lies down, since that will probably distract him and make him jump up again. Say something like "Good dog," and leave it at that until he's at your side and the exercise is completed. In between the practice of this exercise, spend some time calling your dog to you in the ordinary manner. This is so that he won't expect to be dropped every time he's called. If he does, he won't trot toward you briskly, but will hang back, waiting to be told to lie down. It's a very good idea to use the hand signal with this one, because you can then drop your dog at a distance too great for shouting.

## Holding the Dumbbell

Because retrieving is so complicated, it is usually taught by a series of exercises rather than one. This first exercise is to get your dog used to holding something in his mouth when you say so. Simple enough, you might think; but many dogs who are perfectly content to sit and come when you give the command aren't at all content to have you telling them what to do with their mouths. Either they resent your putting anything in, or they refuse to relinquish the object when commanded. Since the mouth and teeth are a dog's major defensive weapon, it's not so surprising that dogs aren't as willing to let people tell them what to do with their jaws as they are with their paws. But as soon as you can convince your dog that it won't hurt him in any way to carry a dumbbell or rolled-up newspaper, he'll be as willing to learn this trick as anything else.

What works for you in teaching this exercise is that the dog naturally carries things around in his mouth all the time. Where else is he going to carry anything, with all four feet in use for walking? If you intend to teach advanced obedience, you must start to watch for this action, and reward it when you see it. You can introduce the training object among his toys, but you should make no distinction at first. Praise him for carrying any object, and praise him if he releases it to you when you ask for it. Again, we don't advise trying to train the dog when he's chewing on a bone. For some reason, probably their memories of the wild, dogs, even well-fed ones, are superdefensive about their bones. Never ask your dog to give up a bone to you; rather, ask for one of his toys or the training object if he happens to take it in his mouth. After a while, you can start offering an object to the dog. Once again, give him a great deal of praise when he takes it. You should begin to accompany this action with the command "Take it," so that your pet starts to associate behavior with words.

Once the dog is fairly comfortable with the notion of his trainer's putting things into his mouth and asking for them back, you can narrow your work to just the training object. Put the object in his mouth, holding your other hand under his chin, if necessary, to be sure he doesn't spit it out. Give the command "Take it"; then, after a minute or two, remove the object and tell the dog, "Out." If you've done your pre-training, this will be a painless business, but now you have to make sure that the dog takes the object every time you tell him. If your dog won't give up the object immediately, don't get into a tug-of-war with him. It's very easy to press a dog's jaws apart by pushing the skin on either side of his back teeth. Do this gently while you give the command "Out." As soon as the dog relaxes his grip, take the object and reward the dog with a lot of petting and praise. If your dog refuses to get a good grip on the object, try tapping it a bit to make it wiggle. He'll probably clamp down on the object reflexively. Don't let him hold the object too long at this point, since the idea of the exercise is to practice taking and releasing.

# Picking the Object Up

This exercise uses the same command as the previous one: "Take it." But now the dog is expected to reach for the object by himself, instead of having you place it in his mouth. What you'll probably notice is that as you repeat the command and offer the object to the dog, he'll start opening his mouth to receive it. As soon as you see this, praise him. If you do it right, you can lead the animal by slow degrees to pick the object up all by himself on command. Just remember the end you have in mind, and reward the dog for every step he takes that brings him closer to the goal. If he opens his mouth to take hold of the object, praise him. If he sticks his neck out a bit to take the object, more praise. You may find that the first time you leave the object on the ground and give the command, Oliver snatches it right up. In any case, this exercise proceeds naturally out of the first one if you only have a bit of patience.

You may find that you have to help the dog on this exercise for quite a while. Helping consists of slipping the dumbbell into his mouth when he reaches for it. If he won't reach for it at all, you'll have to backtrack to the point where you hold the dumbbell and all he has to do is extend his neck ever so slightly to win your praise.

Many trainers seem to have a great deal of difficulty teaching dogs to fetch and carry on command. It's probably for this reason that only advanced obedience trials require this exercise. The old-style way to train a dog to retrieve was simply to force him to it time after time until he gave in. We obviously do not believe this to be the most effective way. Instead, we recommend progress by slow increments to the desired goal. Training should not be a contest between you and the dog, in which the real object is to humiliate the animal. Instead, it should be an application of superior reasoning power—yours—to the problem of making an animal conform to human standards. It is no more helpful to force or punish a dog than it is to kick the TV set when it malfunctions. Just the same, it is true that retrieving, jumping, trailing, and scent discrimination are harder to teach than basic obedience. Unless you actually enjoy working with your dog, or find it economically necessary to give him advanced training, you should probably be content with simple obedience.

## Carrying an Object

This exercise is to be taught not in sequence with picking up an object, but simultaneously with it. When your dog has got used to holding the training object in his mouth, he will inevitably carry it with him sometimes, even if only for a few steps. When he does—whenever he does—give him full measure of rewarding praise. Then take the object away from him with the command "Out," and praise him some more. You should do this many times informally before you try to work him on the exercise. When you think the dog is comfortable about carrying the training object, try putting it in his mouth (or telling him to pick it up himself, if he's that advanced) and backing off a few steps. Call the dog to you, and when he comes, if he doesn't drop the dumbbell, reward him. If he does drop the dumbbell, pick it up and give it back to him with the command "Take it." After he can do this consistently, make him walk with you, at heel position, carrying the object until you take it from him. The only humane way to treat him when he drops the dumbbell is to pick it up and give it to him again. With some dogs, it works well to tell them emphatically that that's not what you want. "No" is usually sufficient, but try to keep annoyance and anger out of your voice. If your dog is very sensitive to your disapproval, he'll get the message. If he isn't, there's no use trying to impress him. Better to rely on his sensitivity to your approval, something he wants and needs.

If you want to enter your dog in obedience trials, you have to teach him not to chew on the training object while he's carrying it. Furthermore, if he's going to be a contestant in a recognized AKC competition, he'll have to carry the dumb-bell. No toys, balls, or rolled-up newspapers are allowed in regulation meets. If you're training for your own pleasure, let the dog learn on any object he likes. But if you want to compete, it will have to be the dumbbell, and Inky will have to learn to like it. The usual way to stop a dog from gnaw-ing on the object he's supposed to be carrying is to make it uncomfortable for him to do so. One way that seems to work well for us is to glue a strip of Velcro closing material along the stem of the dumbbell. This is just a bit prickly, so he doesn't really feel like gumming the darn thing. If he persists in spite of this dissuasion, try other methods of distracting him so that he startles a bit and stops mouthing. But don't be too startling, or he might drop the dumbbell altogether, which would be a setback.

About time. Simple obedience can be attained by most owner–dog teams in the 21 days outlined in our plan. Ad-vanced obedience is much more of an individual problem. It all depends on how successful you have been in establishing a good training relationship with your dog, how patient you are, and whether or not you really like dog training. It also depends to some extent on the personality of your dog, though if you have trained him carefully since puppyhood, he's likely to have a calm and agreeable disposition.

# Fetch

This is what the previous exercises have been leading up to, since it's just a combination of these tricks in sequence. Throw out the training object, whatever the dog is used to carrying, and tell him to "Take it." If he has learned the other exercises, he'll go out after the object, pick it up, and hold it in his mouth. Then call him to you, and tell him to sit in front of you. Let him hold the object for a minute or two before you take it from him, giving the command "Out." After the whole exercise is completed, reward him. If the dog is reluctant to go out after the object, you go with him. Point to the object and give him the command to "Take it" once again. You may find that although Fifi performed all the parts of the fetch separately, she balks at the combination. If this happens, it just means she's in for a little review. You must go back to putting the object in her mouth, for instance, if she won't pick it up readily by herself.

In the beginning, don't throw the object very far: maybe five or six feet. Later, when the dog is more steady on every part of the exercise, you can throw it as far as your arm will let you. Don't worry if the dumbbell falls out of sight. It's good practice for the dog to have to look for the object a bit, especially if you intend to go on to teach him scent discrimination and trailing. The fetch is one exercise that works much better with some breeds than with others. Retrievers, of course, are specifically bred for this one talent. And if you don't think that genetic makeup can be much of a factor, just try tossing an object out in front of a retriever puppy. Now compare what he does with what a cocker spaniel or, better yet, a terrier will do. Somehow, without ever having been shown, the retriever puppy knows what to do. He'll fetch the object and fling it at your feet, fairly begging you to throw it again. We once had a retriever who was so single-minded about this game that he scoured the neighborhood for suitable objects, bringing home toys and household items from blocks away. All of these he piled in front of our door, as if to say, "Look at what there is to choose from. *Now* don't you want to play?" The retriever puppy has just the right attitude. Fetching is a game, and you want him to treat it as such. There's no prettier sight in the world of training than to see a dog retrieve happily, bouncing back with the object in his mouth, filled with obvious pride.

In order to get your dog to fetch in this spirit—even if he's not a retriever—you have to treat the exercise as a game. To let your dog have some fun at it, run out with him yourself to get the object. Most dogs like nothing better than to really run alongside their masters, just as they would run with the leader in a wild pack. Don't bother with this if your dog seems to think fetching is fun, but use it liberally for the dog who isn't much interested at first. After he starts to really like the game, you can sober him up a bit by making him wait until you say so before he goes after the dumbbell. Actually, all training exercises should be made pleasurable for the dog whenever possible. The whole idea of our training method is to arrange the environment in such a way that the very most pleasant thing for the dog to do is what you command him. The best way to do this is to make the exercise truly pleasurable and rewarding through the liberal use of praise and love. The second-best way is to make every alternative so unattractive that he will choose to do what you want him to. This latter—the use of negative reinforcement—works in dog training only as long as the dog doesn't see the punishment as a hostile gesture on your part. That's why you must manipulate the environment, or at least manipulate the dog, so that he doesn't see that it's you throwing the water, banging the can, tossing the noisy chains. He has no resentment about the fact that he gets wet when it rains, for example. He can see very well that the weather is an entirely impersonal phenomenon. But he will resent persons or animals who treat him badly. In our experience, bad treatment includes trying to force a dog to obey you. This hurts his feelings, at least, even if it doesn't cause actual physical pain.

# Jumping

Because advanced obedience awards are given to dogs who can leap over hurdles, jumping is usually taught as jumping *over* something. But it's really more useful than that, even to the ordinary pet owner who has no interest in dog shows. If your dog will jump on command, imagine how much easier your trips to the veterinarian will be. Just tell him, "Up!" and watch him leap onto the examining table. Your vet will be impressed, you can be sure. It is for this exercise that you have acquired the jumping stick. (You have, haven't you?) Although jumping is fun for most dogs, you have to show them what you want at first, since they are always surprised by any request that requires them to take all four feet off the ground. Take the jumping stick on a walk, along with the dog, and simply stick it out in front of you and the dog while you're walking along. Try not to break stride, and don't let the dog stop, either. This is a good trick in which to train with the leash, at least in the beginning. You have to step over the stick first, to demonstrate what you want Willy to do. Of course, since you're holding the stick, you can't completely climb over it, but just lift up your left leg as if you were going to. At the same time, give a quick pull on the leash and the command to "Jump," or just "Up."

The thing to avoid, if you teach the jumping exercise with

the dog on a leash, is hauling the poor fellow over the stick or hurdle by his neck. Give a quick, sharp pull on the leash—purely as a signal—and then stop. Let the line go slack again, and the dog will take the barrier by himself. It's very likely that the dog will balk the first few times you put the stick in front of him, but don't punish him for it. Just repeat the whole business a few steps farther on—pretending to climb over the stick yourself each time—until he has a clear idea of what's expected of him. Once he finds out that the stick is no threat, he'll probably jump willingly.

The jump is a bit harder to teach than basic obedience, simply because you aren't as likely to see the dog leaping over something as you are to find him spontaneously sitting, say, or lying down. Because of this, it's harder to find occasions for praising him. You'll have to create the occasions yourself, by providing things for the dog to leap. After your pet has jumped with you a few times and seemed to enjoy it, why not set up a hurdle in his yard or wherever he normally plays? Watch him, and if you ever see him jump over the bar, offer all the admiration and praise you can muster. It's a slower game this way, but more satisfying for both you and the animal. It's nothing but a pleasure to see your dog learn to do what you want for the sheer joy of pleasing you. Strangely enough, most owners feel that they've worked harder for less when they force a dog to perform than when they've coaxed him with loving-kindness. Sure, you can make the dog jump by pulling him over obstacles by his neck; but isn't it better to have him leaping just for the pleasure of the jump and your praise, even if it takes a few days longer for the dog to catch on?

In any case, once the dog has the basic idea firmly in his mind, you can start to raise the stick a bit higher. In the beginning, about a foot off the ground is high enough, even for a big dog. Later, you can stop stepping over it yourself, and raise the stick to two feet or more. You should still suggest to the dog what you want him to do, by leaning into the jump with your left shoulder (if the dog walks at your left heel) or with an arm gesture. Now speed up your walk so that the two of you are moving at a slow trot. There's no use trying to hide the stick from the dog, and no purpose in trying to surprise him. Let him know that you're going out for a jumping exercise and he'll probably be all prepared for it. As soon as Charlie loses his fear of something new, he'll no doubt be an avid jumper. Most dogs are. You'll have to watch him at this point so that his enthusiasm doesn't carry him away. Be sure you make him heel both before and after the jump. If he tends to break away after jumping, or to tug on the leash throughout the whole exercise, make him sit after he has jumped. If even this doesn't work, give him the command to "Lie down" just as he finishes the jump. You can also practice making him jump back the other way over the stick. Vary the routine so that he doesn't get bored or start anticipating you.

Telling him to lie down after each jump is even more useful once you start him jumping without the leash. Because jumping is such an enjoyable experience for most dogs, once they get the hang of it they feel exuberant and free. This is great for morale, of course, but bad for discipline. To keep George in line, make him lie down every time, and put him back on the leash if he runs away from you after jumping. Keep raising the stick a little higher until it's level with whatever you've chosen to use as a permanent hurdle.

This is also a good time—once you're sure he likes to jump—to have your dog start carrying his dumbbell with him when he takes the leap. Just give him the dumbbell (or whatever you use) and command him to "Carry" while the two of you are walking toward the stick or hurdle. He'll probably forget and drop the object the first few times, just because he can't keep so many things in his mind at the same time. Don't scold him, but just pick up the dumbbell and put it back in his mouth. After a while, when it isn't all so new to him, he'll be able to do both tricks without thinking twice. Working dogs, such as bloodhounds and sheepdogs, must do many more than two things at once, sometimes out of sight of the master and with his last command as their only guide. They do it, most of them, very well, and with no other training than the kind your dog is getting from you. More extensive, to be sure, but step-by-step just the same. They have all learned the same way, and your dog will learn too.

There are some times in the course of any kind of learning when the forward progress just seems to stop. Lots of educators have investigated learning "plateaus," and there is still no comprehensive explanation for them. Some people think that plateaus are reached when the tasks suddenly go up in difficulty. If this is true, our training method is one that will help minimize dead spots. This is because we advocate very gradual acceleration, moving just one tiny step at a time toward the ultimate goal. At first, we praise an animal if he does anything remotely like what we want the final behavior to be. Later, when he is more consistent, we narrow our sights, and praise only behavior that comes very close to the final goal. But all this is done by gradual degrees. Both the trainer and the dog edge toward perfect performance very slowly, and always in a positive way. If you, the trainer, get impatient with this inching toward the final aim of your work, remember that this is really the fastest way to get just what you want, without at the same time teaching the dog bad habits (such as resentment) that you later have to un-teach.

Impatience is one of the biggest problems with amateur animal trainers. But remember, it's never (really, never) the dog who loses his patience. It's always that creature of superior reason, the human being. If you do find yourself in

periods of no progress, don't give up. You should work with
your dog every day. But don't think of it as a race to accomplishment. Rather, tell yourself that you're just putting the
dog through his paces, keeping him in shape. You'll have to
do just that—work the animal regularly—even after you've
decided he doesn't need to learn any more tricks. Very likely,
if you and Butch have got this far, you'll never come to the
end of your training. You both must like working together, or
you would have stopped with basic obedience. And there'll
always be something new to teach yourself and your dog. But
you'll have to learn to deal with the slow times if they come.
Talk yourself into believing that it's just exercise time, just
a good habit for you and your pet. One fine day, just when
you've decided he's washed up as a student, Dandy will surprise you by waking up as eager to learn new things as he
was the day you brought him—decidedly wet behind the
ears—home from the kennel.

When you first start to work your dog with permanent
hurdles instead of a broomstick, you may be dismayed to
see His Eagerness slinking under the bar instead of leaping
high as before. If you're prepared for this lapse, you can
resist the urge to scold him. Be firm, and lead him back to
the hurdle to try again. You'll have to return for a while to
the old trick of stepping over the barrier yourself with your
left leg. Don't make the bar too high at first, for both the
dog's sake and yours. You might find yourself throwing a
hip out in your enthusiasm for the bar hurdle. If you do the
first hurdle work on a leash, and that's definitely the easiest
way for you, have Gabby take the hurdle, stand on the other
side, and then jump back to where you are. If you aren't
training the dog for competition, you'll probably find it easier
to dispense with the bar hurdle for training purposes and
use just a solid hurdle—like a section of fence—that the
dog can't sneak under.

If you do want to compete, you should know that the regulation height for show jumping is twice the shoulder height of the dog. In practice, your hurdles should eventually be raised to this height. Don't do it all at once, or you'll surely encounter resistance. Once the dog is a willing jumper at the lower levels, start raising the barrier by slow degrees. In the case of the solid hurdle, just add another plank to the fence. If the dog balks, lower the bar again until he takes it without protest. Once he can jump as high as you want him to, practice working him with the dumbbell or other training object in his mouth. By this time he'll be used to carrying on the jump, and will no doubt be very pleased with himself about it all.

In all this work, we seldom specify how many trials it will take you and the dog to accomplish any one exercise. This is because learning times vary so widely among breeds and also among different trainers. In general, two weeks of twenty minutes a day should be more than enough for an obedient dog to learn any of the more advanced exercises in this chapter. You may find, especially if your working relationship with your pet is excellent, that the actual times are much shorter. Two weeks is an average and includes steps that are fairly easy to teach—like jumping—averaged with more difficult work, such as retrieving the dumbbell. Dogs, being clever animals, are capable of one-trial learning. This means that they can get a lesson once and for all on the first presentation. But in order for any experience to have so deep an effect on the first trial, it has to be something of a shock. If you were to use devices to stun or frighten the dog, and present him with the choice of jumping, for example, or getting an electric jolt, there's no doubt that the dog would jump. The farther you move away from such scare tactics, the more trials it will take the dog to catch on. You have the advantage, however, of having him associate pleasure with performing for you, rather than recalling it with pain and fear. Since most of us keep dogs for pleasure in the first place, it seems only reasonable that we confine our training methods to the pleasant.

# Retrieving and Jumping

This is really what all the fuss has been about. The exercises of jumping and retrieving on the flat are now to be combined to show your dog how to jump over an obstacle, retrieve an object, and jump back to where you are. It's amazing how much pleasure this accomplishment can give a trainer, probably because it's the first really complex series of actions your dog has mastered. Although it takes much longer to train a dog to retrieve over a hurdle than to teach him a simple sit, it offers much greater rewards for the patient teacher. When you feel that your dog can take a command and carry it out over time and even over physical barriers, you feel for the first time like part of a real working team. There is an understanding now between you and the dog that makes him more than just a pet, you more than just a pet owner.

To teach the dog to retrieve after a jump, start out again with your barrier at a fairly low level. This is advisable even if the dog has been jumping obstacles that are twice his shoulder height. At first, you'll have to give him a lot of commands that he's not used to executing together, and it's wise to make it as easy on him as possible. To really do it right, you should have your dog on the sit-stay in front of the low hurdle. Throw out his favorite training object, then give him the command to jump. When he's on the other side, tell him to take the object. You may find that you have to actually put the dumbbell in his mouth, the way you did when you were first teaching him to take it. Don't be dismayed at this seeming regression. Remember that the dog is used to doing these tricks in isolation, and he may be a bit confused by having them all thrown at him at once. Don't be reluctant to go all the way back to the beginning of a lesson, if necessary, until Eddie feels perfectly comfortable with the whole combination.

After your dog has picked up the training object, tell him to jump back over the hurdle to where you are. He'll be used to this, since you've taught him to jump both ways when you introduced the hurdles. If he balks, pat the top of the jump, and coax him to make the return. If he starts to sneak around the end of the hurdle, discourage him with a "No." If he persists in walking away, rather than making the return jump, try training him on the leash, just as you did when you were first teaching him to jump. Be sure not to stand directly behind the jump when you're trying to get a dog to leap toward you. If he thinks he's going to crash headlong into you, he'll certainly be reluctant.

During the time you're teaching him to retrieve over the hurdle, you'll also want to teach your dog to respond to fewer commands in this exercise. It is inconvenient and distracting to keep telling Fritzi each individual part of the operation. Try eliminating some of the commands, until just the "Jump" and "Carry," or "Fetch," are left. After he understands the exercise well, there should be only one or two words passing between you and the dog. Just as in the original jumping lessons, you should be sure your dog is clearing the hurdle at any given height before you raise the bar. If he's scrambling up the side and flopping over, he doesn't have enough confidence yet at that height, and you should lower the bar again. It may still help him for you to demonstrate what you want by throwing one leg over the bar, or at least inclining your shoulder into the jump. If the dog can clear the jump very well but insists on trying to sneak around the end instead of making the return jump, you may have to get out your old rattling chains to throw at him. Even better, get a friend to throw the chains, so that the dog won't suspect you of trying to do him harm.

We should mention here that obedience trials require a dog to jump over a series of long, low hurdles as well as over a high hurdle. If you intend to compete with the dog, get a copy of the regulations for an American Kennel Club obedience competition, and study what your dog will be expected to do to win any of the three obedience distinctions the AKC offers. We will not discuss the long jump here, since the method of training is so obviously similar to that of the high jump. Usually, this is rather an easy variation for the dog to master, because he's already used to the command to jump. Remember not to ask too much of your dog on the long jump. He can jump only so far—depending on his size. To ask more of him is to demand the impossible, which can only create animosity between animal and trainer.

It's also a good idea to get the dog used to fetching and carrying articles other than the one you've always used in training. By this time, your pet should be very good at "Take it" and "Carry," and it won't be a source of confusion to him if you ask him to obey these commands with something other than the everlasting dumbbell. In fact, if he's like many dogs we've known, he'll actually be grateful for the change. Even though a well-trained dog comes to think of the dumbbell or whatever as his object, he's proud to demonstrate that he understands the commands and can perform with any object you give him. And your pride as a trainer will increase, too, when you see that he really knows how to fetch, away from the training environment. Old Gus really does understand the commands, by the way, as you can prove to yourself by inserting them into longer phrases or sentences. Say, "Gus, old fellow, why don't you jump over the hurdle there and carry back the glove that I've thrown out there for you?" As long as he hears "Jump" and "Carry," Gus will do just what you ask, disregarding all the words he doesn't understand. There's no particular reason for tossing in all those extra words, unless maybe you want to impress guests with how much of your ordinary conversation the dog supposedly understands. We mention it only to point out that once the dog is thoroughly familiar with a command, he'll obey it no matter where it occurs.

As you vary the objects you ask the dog to fetch, put in some that are bound to be unappealing, just to test the animal for steadiness. He won't like, for example, fetching a tin can, but he'll do it. There are enough stories of hunting dogs taught to bring back baby ducklings in their mouths unhurt to show you that dogs can be perfected on the retrieve to almost any degree. One of our dogs was trained by his owner, an experimental scientist, to carry newborn baby mice in his mouth, without ever taking a chomp. The truth is, dogs are willing to go to just about any lengths to please you, as long as you have the patience to train them slowly and lovingly.

# Tricks and Fancy Stuff

There are two reasons that most people want to go beyond basic obedience and advanced obedience. The first is that they want their pets to perform tricks for the entertainment of family and friends. The other is that they want to train a real working dog, either for show purposes or for work in the field. People in this second category include hunters, farmers, policemen, military people, and detectives. But they also include a lot of people who just want the pleasure of having trained a real utility dog. You may not have any real use in your daily life for a dog who can find a lost person from the smell of his shoe, but what an accomplishment to have such a dog, trained by you! Nor is there any real utility in having a dog who can sit up and beg or shake hands. But such tricks are often a great pleasure for animal and master alike, perhaps because they provide something more that human and dog can do together.

## Shaking Hands

This one is so easy that a lot of dogs do it without being taught. Your dog definitely doesn't have to be a graduate of hurdle work to learn this one. In fact, it's the first trick taught to many puppies, and it seems to give pet owners a lot of pleasure. It's best, in teaching this trick, to train the dog on a table, unless he's of a very large breed. At first, you'll just set him up on the table (or command him to jump up, if he's schooled in advanced obedience) and pet him gently. Be patient, and wait until he lifts his paw, even slightly. But wait for the dog to make the move. When he does, take the paw, shake it, and praise the dog vigorously. It takes only about twenty or thirty repetitions like this before the dog knows the trick. Be sure to tell him "Shake," or "Shake hands," every time he does it. Of course, you can practice shaking hands with him anywhere, and it won't be very long before he'll respond perfectly every time.

## Rolling Over

Like all the household tricks, this one is a cinch for a dog who has been through the 21-Day Basic Obedience

Course. If he is already totally reliable on the lie-down, he's halfway there. You can approach the trick by having the dog lie down, then playing with him on the grass or rug. Eventually, he'll accomplish a complete roll. When that happens, reinforce. Don't confuse him about the seriousness of the down-stay, however. Make it clear that this is a different set of circumstances, with a different, more playful mood. Once he learns the command "Roll over," he'll understand that these are two separate exercises. Like shaking hands, this is even easier to teach most dogs than basic obedience. That's because it's fun for most dogs to do these tricks. Repeat the exercise until the dog will do it reliably, even if he's not in the mood. But don't try to show him by turning him over yourself. As always, wait until the dog himself makes the move, then reinforce it with praise and petting.

# Catch

This is a flashy trick, but one that depends heavily on eyesight. Except for the sight hounds, such as the Afghan, the greyhound, and the whippet, most dogs don't see nearly as well as they hear or smell. Lots of dogs don't seem to be able to see an object that's been tossed to them until just before it drops in front of their noses. If your dog is one of those who have trouble with this, it will take somewhat longer to teach this trick than most others. The dog has to learn from experience where to expect the thrown object to be, since he can't really see it for himself. This means lots and lots of trials, maybe more than a hundred, before the two of you can really play catch. The best way to teach this trick is just to toss the object—usually a ball or a tidbit of food— to the dog and praise him if and when he manages to catch it in the air. Throw the object up in a lazy arc, to give the dog plenty of time either to spot it or to guess where it's going to fall. Start the lessons with the dog in a standing position. Later, if you want, you can combine catching with fetching, so that the dog runs out to catch the ball, like a running back going out for a forward pass. While people addicted to the military school of dog training find tricks like this a bit frivolous, we have found that many dog owners get more pleasure from being able to play a quick game of catch with little Heidi than from all her prowess on the sit-stay.

Some dogs, notably the retrievers, are more interested in balls and sticks than in anything else. There's no problem teaching these dogs to catch some such training object. But if your dog isn't one of the natural ballplayers, you might try using little pieces of meat or dog biscuits as the training items for catch. Usually, we don't recommend using food in dog training, but here the idea isn't to reinforce with food— just to use it to get the dog's interest. Don't train the dog when he's hungry, particularly, but use tidbits anyway if he's not interested in the game. If he can't see the object coming, he can at least smell it, and that will help.

## Sitting Up

Here's another trick that's best taught with the help of a bit of food. If the dog is reaching for a tidbit, he'll sit up for it quite naturally. Otherwise, you might spend hours or days watching him, and never see him in the right position. In order for you to reinforce the dog's behavior, the behavior has to occur. Here again, food is being used not as a reward, but as an aid in getting the dog's interest. You can easily teach such exercises as the sit and the lie-down just by waiting for the dog to perform them naturally. But a normal dog will not sit up on his hind legs without inducement. Still, this is a very easy trick to teach, because it's not hard for the dog to do, and he doesn't mind, if that's what you like. Once you've got him sitting up, with forepaws off the ground, praise and pet him. Gradually extend the amount of time he stays in this position until he can do it for as long as you like. If you do use food to induce the sit-up, don't be stingy about giving it to him. As soon as he's sat there a reasonable amount of time—thirty seconds or so—pop the tidbit into his mouth, then praise him for his good performance. After a while, you can dispense with the food some of the time. Ichabod will sit up just as readily for your praise.

If you want to, you can go on from here to real circus-type tricks. The dog who has been taught to sit up can be encouraged by the same means to dance on his hind legs. This usually works best with the smaller breeds, by the way. A German shepherd just has too much weight around his shoulders and head to stand comfortably on two legs. But any dog can and will do it, if you want him to. All breeds of dogs can be taught to climb ladders, walk fences, and all manner of behavior not usual to dogs. Like advanced obedience, performance of tricks like these takes somewhat longer to perfect than basic obedience. That's because none of these things is something a dog is likely to do on his own. He sits or lies down or follows his master quite naturally, most of the time. The only trick with those exercises is to steady him up—make sure he'll do each of them every time you tell him. But more advanced training goes somewhat against the grain, and it will take longer to convince old Tessie that you seriously want her to do that. We don't discuss performance-type tricks in detail here because the demand among ordinary pet owners is relatively small. Most people don't have enough of an audience waiting to see Kinky perform to justify elaborate circus training. But if you want such a specialized dog, we can say from experience that it's entirely within the capabilities of the patient amateur trainer to teach all the tricks that we've named here. If you have the desire and the consistency, you can teach your pet any trick that a circus dog can do.

# Utility Training

Although this kind of training is usually regarded as a more serious business than sitting up or dancing on the hind legs, the degree of difficulty is really very much the same. Maybe utility training is more solemnly thought of because it grew out of the way dogs were trained who were necessary in their masters' work. In order to really prepare your dog properly for utility training, you should follow the courses in basic and adavnced obedience first. If you do, utility training will be just an elaboration on what the dog already knows. If you haven't already put your dog through the course in advanced obedience training, go back to the early part of this section and follow the preliminary exercises there. You can't teach him to look for a lost article, for example, until he knows the simpler idea of retrieving. Trailing is really the most general case of many different kinds of useful work dogs can do—from bringing in the flock to searching for a lost person. If you teach Morris the basic skill, it can be adapted later to cover your particular needs.

In the remainder of this section, we will discuss the general concepts of utility training. If you want to enter your trained dog in obedience trials, you should attend several such trials, and talk to the judges about exactly what they look for when rating obedience dogs. Study the American Kennel Club rules, and read material specially designed to teach you how to train a dog for competition. Many judges, for example, want you to train the dog to sit in front of you after the completion of each exercise. But if you don't wish to enter your dog in competitions, you might very well still want him to learn advanced utility exercises. A dog trained in scent discrimination and trailing is an advantageous companion on hunting trips, farms, or tracking work of any kind. Or perhaps you just want the pleasure of working with your dog and seeing him perform.

# Seeking Back

This exercise is preparation for the scent-discrimination and trailing exercises that follow. But "seeking back" is useful in its own right, since it teaches a dog to look for something you have lost. Conceivably, this skill could be useful around the house, though very few people who train their dogs in this activity ever think of making the dog work at it every day. Too many trainers, in fact, never work the dog at all except in preparation for competition. As a result, an animal who is technically highly trained is lacking in common household manners. Once your dog knows how to search for a lost article, be sure he gets some regular practice.

The lesson begins with you and your dog walking, the dog at heel position. Carry with you the article that the dog will be required to find. In the beginning, the article should be something that feels good in the mouth—not metal or glass. Behind the dog's back drop the test article, and keep walking with him in a straight line for at least another thirty feet. The dropped article should be something that belongs to you, such as a glove, and has not been recently laundered of your scent. When you are some distance from the drop, about-face and take the dog off the leash. Then press your right hand up against his nose (your left hand if that's the one you use more) to give him the scent. Then give him the command to "Take it," which he already knows, plus the new direction "Look for it." On the first ten or twenty trials, you should drop the article in plain sight, so that the dog will have no trouble finding it. When you give him the command to "Take it," he may run out with no urging whatever and pick the object up. This is exactly what you want, so call him back to you and praise him profusely. To be properly formal about it, you should take the object out of the dog's mouth and make him go back to the heel position.

If the dog seems confused by your commands, including "Look for it," which he has never heard before, lead him out to where the article was dropped. Just as you did when you were teaching him to retrieve, you should point to the article and repeat, "Take it," as well as saying, "Look for it." Until he gets the point, you may have to lead him back to the "lost" article every time. Don't lose patience with him just because he already knows how to retrieve. This is a new situation with new demands, and he may not make the right associations at first. After you're certain that the dog understands what's wanted of him, try making a turn before you let him off the leash to seek back. Then make several turns. Go a bit farther away from the article every time, but don't hide it from him until the dog is completely successful at finding an object dropped in the open. Just as in every other exercise, the idea here is to build the dog's confidence every step of the way, so that when he approaches a new task his confidence is high, and he doesn't feel threatened. Don't try to shortcut the training by skipping any of the intermediate steps, and don't rush the dog through them for the pleasure of seeing him do the whole trick. Your quest for immediate gratification may backfire and send you back to the beginning to correct mistakes. Always keep in mind that it is much harder to un-train mistakes than to train an exercise properly the first time.

When you do start hiding the object, it will be another point of confusion for the dog. It may take you some time to convince him that he must hunt for it until he finds it, even if the hunt isn't easy. If you have put him through all the preliminaries with sufficient time and patience, he'll have the stick-to-itiveness to persist until he comes up with the object. Don't forget that on each and every trial, you must let him smell your hand again. Of course, he may be seeking back mostly with his eyesight, especially in the early stages of training. But when the object isn't in plain sight anymore, he'll have to start relying on his keen sense of smell. If you've been reminding him all the time of which scent (the most familiar one—yours) he is to seek, it will come naturally to him to start depending on his nose. In the more advanced stages of his seek-back training, the dog should recover all kinds of objects—not just gloves and soft things. The only requirement should be that you have handled the object and it has your scent. It can be of glass, metal, plastic, or any material, once the dog is fairly steady in finding soft objects. This is because, even as you and I, a dog would prefer to have something soft in his mouth.

## Scent Discrimination

For this exercise, you'll need a whole collection of scented and unscented articles. These can be things like wooden clothespins, keys, gloves, handkerchiefs, scarves, pocketbooks, and even empty bottles. First, you should have two or three of each kind of object. Divide the objects into two groups. The first group will be handled by you regularly. This will be the scented collection. The second group should be thoroughly washed, then handled only with a pair of tongs. Somebody else might touch the articles, but never the trainer. The best way, especially in the beginning, is not to let *anybody* touch the unscented articles. Keep the scented and unscented articles in separate boxes.

On the first trial, use gloves as the articles to be retrieved. Take one from the unscented collection—with the tongs, of course—and put it on the ground a few feet in front of the dog. Your dog is in the sit-stay attitude. Then take a similar glove from the other box and hold it in your hand for a few seconds to be sure it is freshly scented. Put it beside the first glove; then hold your hand over the dog's nose and give him the command to "Take it, Look for it." If he goes for the objects and immediately picks out the scented one, rejoice. A good first trial makes your job easier. But if he starts to pick up the unscented article, tell him, "No" in a firm voice. This should make him drop the article, but if he doesn't, make him give it to you and, still handling it with the tongs, put it back on the ground. Point to the scented article, and encourage the dog to pick it up. If necessary, put the scented glove into his mouth the way you did when you were first teaching him to retrieve. This time, he'll catch on much more quickly.

On succeeding trials, watch the dog closely, and praise him when he even approaches or sniffs at the scented glove. When teaching dogs, or people, for that matter, the quickest way to get them to learn is to make it absolutely crystal-clear what you want them to do. At the beginning of any new lesson, you must remember to praise the dog for any approach to or approximation of the desired behavior. Later, praise only for the exact accomplishment you want, but approach this stage by very gradual degrees. Only when your dog can reliably bring back the correct glove, for example, should you change the placement of the two gloves in any way. After he can choose reliably between the scented and unscented gloves, pull a switch on him by placing two *un-*

scented gloves on the ground, putting out no scented object at all. If he chooses nothing, praise and pat him. But if he makes a move to pick up either of the unscented gloves, tell him, "No," and call him back to you. If this last change in the routine proves baffling to your dog, try setting the scented glove out with the two unscented ones and letting him look for it. He's more likely to have success at this, and then he'll begin to understand what you want. Then try adding other unscented articles with the scented glove. Once he consistently picks the glove, try him again on unscented objects only.

Only when your dog can discriminate reliably between the scented glove and all the unscented objects should you use any other object for your scent. In other words, let him have the security of familiar sight as well as smell. When you think he's ready, switch to some other object that bears your scent, but make it something soft at this point, so that he won't shy away from it on account of feel. When Rusty can bring back the scented pocketbook from among all others, start using the scented clothespin, then the scented cans and bottles. You may be disappointed to see, at this juncture, that your dog fails time after time to bring back the scented article. If this happens, you'll have to start all over again with one scented and one or two unscented things.

When you reach this point in the lesson, you may find yourself losing patience and getting irritable with the dog. If so, stop training right there, and don't hold another session until you feel completely rested and relaxed. It is no more productive to rail at an animal in the advanced stages of training than it is to spank a puppy. But remember this, too: even professionals with long years of training experience will once in a while lose their tempers. If you are harsh with Joker, make it up to him immediately, and the two of you will soon be able to forget it. No trainer is an angel, though some dogs are. If you expect perfection of yourself, you'll be more irritable than if you simply accept your human limitations and try to work around them.

The final phase of the scent-discrimination exercise is the one in which you ask the dog to select the scented from a group of unscented articles, *all of them exactly alike.* This is probably more than any judge at an obedience trial will require of your dog, but it is the ultimate test for steadiness in this skill. The customary item to use is the golf ball, though any articles will do, as long as there is no difference visible to the dogs among them. Handle one object yourself, and mark it for your own identification; be sure to touch the others only with tongs. At a dog show, the judge will expect you to supply a random collection of unscented articles and will give you one to handle. Then the ring steward will take the scented article and place it with the other (unscented) things across the ring, being careful not to touch the scented article himself. If your dog has passed the golf-ball test at home, he should have plenty of confidence to handle the scent-discrimination test in the show ring. Besides, this test is the final signal to you that you really have taught the dog to use his nose, rather than any other sense organ, to seek out the correct object. Since your pet can't talk to you, it is always very satisfying for the trainer to have visible proof that the dog has understood the meaning of a complex lesson.

# Trailing

Trailing by scent is the ultimate service a dog can perform for his master. It is the one thing that a dog can do very well and a person cannot do at all. If he has to, a shepherd can round up his own sheep, and electronic burglar alarms can replace the guard dog. But nothing can substitute for the dog's superior sense of smell. Other animals have it, of course, but what they lack is a willingness to serve men. The dog has both, and it is for this that he has been valued since prehistoric times. It's very likely that dogs were first domesticated to help in the hunt. True, dogs couldn't use weapons, but they had a weapon built in—their tracking ability. The fact that a dog can fetch and carry is wonderful, and it's useful to have him learn the names of common household objects. But his true skill is following the invisible trail left by every individual human or other animal wherever he goes.

Unless you hunt, you probably don't have any economic or sporting reason to own a trailing dog. But the pleasure of teaching your pet this skill and having him perform success-fully is reason enough. When trainer and dog have attained this level of accomplishment, there is a closeness between them that is unique among relationships. One Airedale of our acquaintance did this for his family: Every morning he would follow the children to school, with the blessing of all concerned. Sooner or later, one child would discover that he had forgotten a vital lunch box, hat, or notebook. Often, nobody would know whether the article in question had been left on the kitchen table or dropped along the way. In either case, Peter, as the dog was called, would be instructed to "Look for the mitten," or whatever had been lost. This dog had a working vocabulary of at least five hundred words. Peter would trot off, following the often winding trail that the children had taken on the way to school. Invariably, he would return with the lost object, either found along the way or picked up from the hands of a confidently waiting mother at home. Even though Peter was never required to participate in a hunt or track a lost person in his life, his utility training was absolutely invaluable to his family. And beyond that, each and every family member was so proud of Peter and his abilities that he might well have been just another of their bright, lovable children. There is no better situation for the well-being of a domesticated dog than to live in a family that loves and admires him. And there is nothing that can make you more pleased with your pet than the feeling that the two of you really have a mutual understanding.

The difference between seeking back, which your dog will already know, and trailing, which he is now to learn, is that in looking for a lost article, the dog is allowed to wander wherever he wishes in his search. When trailing, he must learn to follow—with his nose as his only guide—the exact path that a person has taken. At the end of that path is a lost article, which the dog is expected to retrieve, just as in the seeking-back exercises.

Please keep in mind that while it is much keener than yours, the dog's sense of smell is not a miraculous extra attribute. It is genuinely hard work for a dog to concentrate on following a scent across a long stretch of ground. If ever you have been impatient in training your dog, this is the time to repress your exasperation. In this exercise particularly, Happy deserves all your understanding. Work him for very short periods, even after he seems to be getting on well. It isn't only that there is frustration for you; there will also be fatigue and irritation for him. This may well be the only exercise in standard obedience training that is as hard on the dog as it is on the master. In most obedience training, you have been learning far more than the dog. The demands on him have been to do things he would do anyway, more or less regularly. But seeking back and trailing require the utmost thought a dog is capable of. It's as if you tried to take an exam in advanced mathematics every day for five or six hours.

So with the dog's limitations in mind, you can lay your first trail. To do this, simply walk across a large field. A concrete area won't serve for this training, so if you live in the city you'll have to find a large public park, or take the dog out into the country to train him. This is because, in order to make the scent accessible, you must scuff up the dirt periodically. This is what dogs themselves do, usually after urinating, to leave trails for other dogs to follow or avoid. You must have seen this behavior at some time. Perhaps you thought the dog was trying to conceal the area on which he had relieved himself. Just the opposite is true. He's trying to mark the spot for others whose sense of smell is as acute as his. You must also wear leather-soled shoes when you lay the trail. Rubber or composition soles won't retain your scent and transfer it to the ground. If it's summer, you might wear leather moccasins, especially if they're old ones, thoroughly impregnated with your scent.

Get one of the dog's familiar scented articles, or maybe two. Stay away from tricky items like golf balls, or objects the dog doesn't especially like to pick up, such as glass bottles. A leather glove is always a good bet. Besides the article to be dropped, you should carry some sticks or other markers so that you can see the trail you've made. You, after all, couldn't sniff out the right track. It's common to use stakes five or six feet tall, with pieces of white cloth tied to the top as flags. This is for your benefit and won't be noticed by the dog. Remember, his eye level is much lower than yours, and his angle of vision smaller. If you don't have any such tall sticks lying around, lay the trail in an area that provides natural markers such as trees or bushes. For the first trails, simply walk out about one hundred feet in a straight line, and drop several of the dog's familiar scented articles five or six feet apart at the end of the trail. Don't just scatter the objects around, but place them in a straight line, continuing the line of the trail. Then retrace your steps exactly, scuffing up the dirt a bit to make the tracking easier for the dog. Place a stake at the starting point of the trail, and scuff here too.

Now find the dog. He should not have been sitting and watching you lay the trail. Leave him in the house, or in some other part of the field, while you do the trail setting. When the track is all set, fetch the dog and put him on the long line. Lead him to the stake and have him lie down next to it, so that his nose is close to the scuffed-up place where your scent is strongest. Then, pointing to the ground, give him the command to "Look for it." Keep pointing and saying, "That's right. Good fellow. Look for it" until the dog picks up the scent and starts out after the objects. He may not get the point about following the trail. You'll know that he doesn't, because he'll leap out as if he were supposed to do the random search of the seeking-back exercise. When he does this, restrain him with the leash. When he puts his nose to the ground to follow the scent, try to make him forget that he's on the lead at all. Play it out very slowly and gently as soon as you see him following the trail. Tighten it ever so slightly when you see his nose go up and his steps start to wander.

If the dog isn't following the scent, point to the ground as the two of you walk the trail. Encourage him to "Look for it," but don't force his nose into the dirt. Try to coax him to put his head down in your tracks by patting the earth or by any other means to attract his attention to the ground. When he gets to where the articles are dropped, he'll pick one up. When that happens, you must act as though you've just seen an angel. Praise the dog heartily and make a big fuss over him, even if you've had to lead him every step of the way. Then take him back to the starting marker and send him out after another of the scented objects, and keep it up until he has successfully retrieved them all. If you have placed four or five objects, this will be plenty for one lesson. Don't tax the dog's stamina on this exercise, particularly on the first few trials.

In laying trails for a dog to follow with his nose, you must pay attention to the direction of the wind. When you start out, walk against the wind. This means that the wind is blowing directly into your face as you walk. If you go with the wind, it means that the scent will be blown away from the dog as he searches, which makes tracking difficult and sometimes impossible for him. The same is true if there are crosswinds, which may blow the scent several feet away from where the real trail lies.

As the dog becomes more expert at following a straight trail, vary the exercise by making a turn in the course he must follow. Lay the straight trail for a hundred feet or so, place one of your markers, and make a turn. Then go another fifty feet, drop the scented articles, and pace back along the same line. Don't forget to put another of the markers at the outset of the trail. Tracking is much easier for the dog, by the way, if you pick a field that is a little damp, with long grass to catch and hold the scent. Keep the dog on the leash as he tracks, and check him up slightly when he nears the stake that marks the turn. This is to help him get it right the first time, which is a much more effective way to learn than making mistakes and having to have them corrected. If the dog keeps going in a straight line, let him have his head as he circles to pick up the lost scent. He may need some help of the elementary variety, by which we mean that you might have to point the trail out to him if he can't find it after a while. If he is already competent at following a straight trail, it won't be long before he catches on to the fact that it's now the same thing, only with turns. As your pet gets better at the exercise, you can lay longer and longer trails with more than one turn. But if he seems confused by all the variations, and never or seldom finds the lost articles, you may have to go back to the straight trail for a review. This is a general principle in dog training—namely, that if one lesson seems so difficult that the dog usually fails, you retreat to an earlier, simpler level of instruction.

As you get more and more fancy about the trails that you set for your dog, be sure that you don't make two in the same day that cut across the same ground. If he smells your scent going off in two different directions at once, he'll be hopelessly confused. He may refuse to keep tracking at this point, and with every justification. If you want him to learn even this most difficult of lessons with no pain, you have to be careful never to present him with conflicting signals. For the same reason, never let a continuous trail double back on itself. The only exception to this rule about crossing trails is that tracks may cross each other if they are made by two different people. Your dog's sense of smell is so good that he will easily distinguish between your characteristic odor and that of a friend or helper. You can also let the trail get a bit cold without confusing the dog; but don't try him on any trail more than a few hours old. The basic idea of this—and all—training is never to push yourself or the animal to the point of frustration.

The final test of whether your dog has learned the lessons of trailing is to let him lead you. This means that you remove whatever markers you have been using to show you how to direct the dog. Until now, you've been able to check your pet with the line, pulling him up a bit when you see him go past the stakes you have placed. This time, don't put in any markers as you lay the trail, except for the one at the start/ finish. You can even have a friend lay the trail, so that neither you nor the dog has seen where the track goes. You'll be a bit disappointed if the dog gets it wrong, of course, and at first you'll be fearful that he'll botch it up without your help. But when he does get it right, you'll experience a thrill that has to be felt to be understood. You have reached the point of ultimate confidence and trust between man and dog.

# III
# BREAKING BAD HABITS

*Knee dog in chest to stop jumping.*

*Un-teaching a dog* is much harder than teaching him to do the right thing in the first place. This is why we urge early training, at least of common household manners. You should never allow your young dog to get into the habit of doing something that annoys you, thinking you'll cure him of it when you begin formal obedience training. It's possible, but it's much the hardest way. Sometimes, though, in spite of all you can do, the dog does develop bad habits. Maybe he's an older dog who has learned the behavior at his previous home. Or maybe the habits are the kind that any puppy is likely to exhibit full-blown without any warning, such as crying in the night or chewing slippers. Whatever the problem, it should be attacked with vigor as soon as you recognize it.

This is not to say that you should attack your dog. He must be vigorously discouraged from doing the undesirable deed, but not from being a friend to man. This means that you should never punish him. He should not be made to feel that you are hurting him or that you are the source of harm. Sometimes he can be persuaded to replace his bad habits with good ones just for the reward of your love. But if discouragement is in order, be sure that the dog believes the bad consequences came from his act, not from you. There are two tricks for accomplishing this deception. The first, already mentioned, is to distract the dog's attention from his barking or chewing or whatever, then praise him for having stopped. The second is to arrange unpleasant consequences in such a way that the dog feels they came from his actions and not from his master's.

## Staying Alone

The new puppy misses his mother and his littermates. This is almost universal. It won't do to be too harsh on the little fellow the first few nights he's away from all that warm company. Many trainers recommend putting an alarm clock (for the ticking) or a hot-water bottle in the puppy's bed the first night or two. You can try these, though you should be prepared for some crying anyway. It's a perfectly natural way for a little dog to try to find the mother he thinks is lost, and it will fade away after a few nights, especially if he's loved a lot during the day. Like all of the nuisances of puppyhood, it seems as though it's never going to stop, but as soon as it does, you forget how much sleep you lost.

The best way to make sure that you don't lose too much sleep is to start training the puppy to stay alone during the day. His cries will be much less disturbing to you and to your neighbors at two in the afternoon than at two in the morning. While you're still in the house, put the puppy in his bed or the confined space where he usually spends the night. Just go on about your business, and let him cry. If he quiets down after a while, go in to him, praise him, and let him out to play. Don't go in while he is crying, but wait for a break, however brief; that way, the pup gets the impression of being rewarded for doing something he should, rather than having won the battle to get your attention. If you do this for several short periods during the day, the hours of yapping during the night will soon start to decrease. In a week or two, when the puppy is completely used to being in your home, he should sleep soundly in his own bed. Don't make the mistake of letting the dog sleep on *your* bed—not even once—unless you want him to make it his permanent headquarters. If he's going to live with people, the puppy has to learn to stay in his own place, and to stay there without yelping.

After a while, the puppy may be content to stay in another room while you're in the house, but he'll bark when you actually leave. If you get an older dog, this habit is often already established, and it's harder to cure him of it than it is to teach the lesson to a new puppy of eight or nine weeks. Just the same, it can be done. In the case of the dog who cries only when you leave home, you have to convince him that you've gone, but secretly stay to discourage him. Some people work it like this: Let the dog see you getting ready to go out— putting on your coat, picking up your briefcase, putting him away in his place. But instead of actually going, slam the door and stay inside. Or, if circumstances demand it, go out, but stay just outside the door, waiting for the dog to set up his howl. This is a business that requires a lot of patience, and a lot of standing around outside closed doors. But training is a slow, step-by-step affair, and you *need* a great deal of patience. Make up your mind to see every lesson through to the end, and you'll be rewarded with a well-behaved animal who will be welcome anywhere.

When the dog who has been left alone begins to bark and howl, what you must do is create a sudden, loud noise. Rap on the door with a rolled-up newspaper, a metal pie plate, or a stick. One trainer recommends firing blank cartridges at the door, but for most of us this is an extreme measure. The point is to create a tremendous racket that will frighten the dog without giving him the notion that he's being punished by you. We don't recommend that you shout, "Bad dog" or anything of the sort, since he'll know then that it's a reprimand. It's much better if he believes that the crash is in some way bound directly to his noisemaking. You might try throwing a rock against the door of the dog's kennel or room, provided that it won't hurt the building. Please don't go in to the dog and shake him or spank him; that would undo whatever progress you've made with the surprise-racket technique. You may have to spend several minutes waiting for the dog to start fussing, but if you have reason to believe that he's in the habit of barking while you're away, it's best to break him of it early. Most older dogs who bark under these circumstances are ones who have been allowed to get away with murder in their youth. If you want the dog to wait patiently when you go out, make sure you take the time—when you're not in a hurry to get someplace.

# Barking

Besides the troublesome dog who howls or barks when he's left alone, there's the dog who won't stop barking even when people are around. Usually, something touches him off—such as the approach of visitors or a noise in the street —and then he's off on an uncontrollable barking jag that can last ten or fifteen minutes. No owner should let his pet get so out of control as this, and you should discourage this tendency the first instant you notice it. This doesn't mean that the dog is forbidden to bark. That would be like forbidding a fish to swim—both unnatural and useless. You can't take away your dog's bark, except by bizarre surgery, and it would be cruel to try. But every dog should be trained to stop barking when his master gives him the command.

The easiest way to get your dog to stop barking, especially when he is still a pup, is to hold his muzzle closed with your hand. A lot of people never stumble on this simple expedient for shutting a dog up, and they spend months or even years whacking the poor animal on the behind without ever getting the message across. Of course, you shouldn't keep holding the dog's mouth closed for a long time; hold it just long enough so that he gets the point. At the same time that you hold his muzzle, tell him, "Quiet!" in a firm voice. Then let go, and unless he immediately sets up a noise again, praise him for having obeyed you.

An even better method, if you can manage it, is to make

a loud noise behind the dog whenever he starts to bark. A short length of chain is wonderful for the maneuver, because it makes a horrendous clatter when flung to the floor. The trick, once again, is not to be seen by the dog while you're throwing the chain. You might try shutting him in a room, then ringing the doorbell, or whatever usually sets him off. When he starts to bark, throw the chain against his door or cast it behind him on the floor. At the same time, give the command "Quiet!" and then praise him when he stops barking. Repeat the lesson as often as you have to until nothing happens when you ring the bell. If your dog is still a pup, it won't take you very long to cure him of the habit. If not, persistence is the key. Just about the time you begin to think he's never going to learn, the dog will suddenly become obedient. Remember not to punish him, but only to reward him when he does what you wish.

You may have the idea that you want the dog to bark for protection. You may even have thought that he could protect you by biting or attacking intruders. Generally speaking, amateur guard training doesn't work very well. If you try to teach the dog to bark at strangers, he ends up yapping at all your friends and being a nuisance. And never, never try to train an attack dog yourself. This is a dangerous matter, and should be left entirely in the hands of professional trainers. In simple obedience training you're working with your dog's gentlest impulses—his need for love and desire for praise. But attack training aims to bring out just the opposite tendencies in the animal. Do-it-yourself attack training has been known to have tragic results. Such dogs may attack of their own volition someday, and bring grief to you and those around you.

# Chewing

Next to housebreaking, the most bothersome problem about young puppies is their propensity to gnaw on things that were never meant to withstand puppy teeth. Few dog owners have never come home to find their new shoes in tatters or the corners missing from a favorite book. But this sort of thing shouldn't happen more than a time or two in the life of any puppy. You shouldn't assume that the dog will outgrow this habit. While it's true that puppies do go through a period when they need to gnaw, they may keep chewing things up, if nobody tells them not to, well after that phase has passed.

One thing that helps keep your carpet slippers and magazines intact is to give the pup plenty of legitimate chewing objects. He likes bones, of course. Try to be sure that he has one or two good ones all the time. And rubber toys are good, provided they are hard enough to give his teeth some resistance. Be sure that the chewing toys don't look anything like other articles around the house that are not for chewing. Never give a puppy an old shoe of his very own; there is no way he can be expected to discriminate between that shoe and the whole wealth of yummy ones to be found at the bottom of your closet.

If you should be lucky enough to spot the dog starting to chew on something forbidden, try the trick of the crashing chains again, or anything else that will make a loud noise of uncertain origin. You must not give the dog the impression that you're throwing something at him. That will make him shy and fearful. The idea, as before, is to get him to associate unpleasant consequences with the act itself. When the dog stops chewing because he's startled, immediately call him to you and praise him. If you wish, call out, "No" in a sharp tone as you make the noise. But remember to give praise for what the dog has done right—stopping his chewing.

As for what to do when you come home to find the bottoms of your draperies gnawed into a fringe, this is trickier. It would be artificial not to express your disapproval to the dog, and he should know that this activity is expressly forbidden. On the other hand, slapping him around won't do any good, for either of you. When something like this happens, you know that you must make a special effort to break the habit. You may have to spend some time waiting around for the dog to start chewing again, but take the time, and be alert. Sooner or later, he'll try it again, and you'll be ready with your crashing noises and your command of "No!" Another trick to use when you're home is to close the puppy off in a different room. We're not talking about his little sleeping space this time, but another room of the house—one that has at least a few tempting chewables in it. Look in on him often, trying to surprise him just as he begins to do something he shouldn't. He already knows you don't want him to chew things, and when he sees you peeking at him, his guilty conscience will take over. This is good practice for the dog who doesn't like being left alone. This way he'll get used to being shut up sometimes, and won't take his resentment out on you when you really do have to leave him. Since he can't be with you every minute, no matter how much love there is between you, he might as well learn to accept the inevitable with good grace.

# Theft

The dog who steals things is just like the dog who chews, except that the thief doesn't destroy your property, he just removes it. Sometimes such a dog plays with the object he steals, sometimes he hides it, sometimes he does do it dam-age. In any case, this is a habit that should be discouraged as early in puppyhood as possible. When you see your pup even reach for something that isn't his, make one of your loud, distracting noises, and call the dog to you. When he comes, praise him for leaving the stolen object and obeying your command to come. Since you can't watch your pet every minute, you'll have to test him after a while, to be sure he's really learned his lesson. Try putting him alone in a room full of stealable goodies, the same as you would with a puppy or dog who's inclined to chew up things. Peek in every few minutes to see if the dog is taking something that doesn't belong to him. (As we have said, every dog should have his toys—things that really *do* belong to him.) If you catch the dog stealing something, repeat the distraction technique, and call him to you. Then praise, as usual. This kind of training accomplishes two things at once: it breaks the bad habit—in this case, stealing—and it trains the dog to leave off whatever he's doing and come at once when you call. Since you can't anticipate all the naughtinesses your pet may get into in a lifetime, strict obedience to the com-mand "Come!" is your surest way to maintain control at all times.

# Jumping Up

This is one of the worst faults an adult dog can have, if you want your friends and neighbors to like him. You won't have to deal with this very tenacious habit if you don't let it get started in the first place. So don't let your puppy jump up, and you won't have to spend hours and days reprimand-ing your adult dog. Most dog owners seem to think that jumping up is "cute" in the puppy, and they don't begin to see the habit as annoying until the animal suddenly weighs seventy-five pounds and plants a huge pair of filthy paws in the center of their clean white shirt. By this time, it's way too late to take the easy way out.

As soon as your puppy is past the actual infant stage, when he really needs all the love and approval he can get, start to discourage him from jumping up. When he leaps at you, push him gently away, and indicate your displeasure by saying, "No." There's no need, in this or any other training, to punish the dog. It's enough that you don't reward the behavior, and that the pup knows you don't like it. He'll soon turn to other pursuits that have shown promise in bringing smiles and praise his way.

As for the older dog who jumps up, there are several ways of breaking the habit. Like any re-training, this takes a lot longer than early discouragement, but it's very important, and it can be done if you're patient. Older manuals of dog training suggest that you do things like step on the dog's hind feet when he jumps up on you. This would be a painful consequence, all right, but hard to do, and especially hard to do without giving the dog the impression that you're trying to hurt him. If you arrange some consequence for the dog's wrong behavior, it must be done so that it seems to the animal that the pain or noise is the natural result of his actions. If he knows that the fright or the hurt comes from you, he'll just hate you. He won't learn to stop the bad behavior, except as a corollary of his fear of you. This isn't, and never was, a reliable guarantee that he won't do the forbidden things when you're not around, or just when he's so angry at you that he's willing to take his lumps to get your goat.

Traditionally, the advice for people whose older dogs jump up has been to give the animal a knee in the chest. This is good, but you have to be sure to arrange it so that the dog thinks it's *his* fault for banging into your knee. If he sees it as an aggressive move on your part, it will be just another punishment. Negative reinforcement was favored by some animal trainers in the past because it often seems to get dramatic results. Steady, positive reinforcement progresses only one tiny step at a time. It's easy to get discouraged at first, when you can't see that all this patience on your part is doing much good. But negative reinforcement has its hidden consequences that lead to a shy, angry, or badly behaved dog in the long run. Many people never do figure out why their dogs suddenly "go bad," after having been so well trained at first.

In order to work the knee-in-the-chest trick properly, you have to raise your knee exactly at the moment the dog starts his jump. He'll probably have his eyes fixed on your face at this point, having already decided to jump and set his muscles in motion. He won't be watching your legs, especially if he doesn't suspect you of trying to do him harm. Lift your knee with enough thrust to topple the dog over backward, then quickly put both feet back on the ground. The idea is not to let the dog see what you're doing to him. Once again, he gets the notion that the unbalancing is somehow a natural consequence of his having jumped up on you. If you persist, he'll soon decide that the pleasure of throwing himself at people isn't worth the discomfort. And he won't blame you, he'll blame himself.

Many trainers have had great success with the simple expedient of *pushing* the dog over backward when he jumps up. The trouble with this one is that it's easier for the dog to see that it's you doing the pushing. If he blames his problems on you instead of on his own behavior, all the value of the training maneuver is lost. You might find it physically easier to push the dog than to knee him in the chest, and if so, try it this way: As soon as the dog starts his leap, grab him by the forepaws and push him away from you, hard.

He'll lose his balance, or at least he'll have to scramble hard not to. As soon as he regains some composure, he'll look at you to find out what happened, so be sure to arrange yourself in a posture of innocence. On the other hand, don't be so gentle with your push that the dog thinks you're playing. This will have an effect the very opposite of what you want. The dog will jump on you even more, to continue the game. It's better to knock the poor fellow on his back once or twice than to spend a lifetime yelling at him for putting pawprints on your tie.

# Cars

How severe you should be in any training depends in part on the temperament of the dog. If your pup is very shy or skittish, it won't do to be so rough that you frighten him. One exception to this rule is running into the street. Often, an animal doesn't get a second chance to learn the lesson of the oncoming automobile. The habit of chasing cars is one of the most dangerous and frightening a dog can form. Like all other bad habits, it's easier for everybody if the dog never has a chance to begin. One well-known trainer solves this problem with a new puppy as soon as the dog is old enough to walk in the street. He takes the dog for a walk, without the leash, and lets the animal wander at will. Sooner or later, the pup will step into the street, and when that happens, pow! The trainer, standing behind the dog, gives him a swat on the rump with all the force he can muster. Once again, it's extremely important not to let the dog see you doing this, or he'll become terrified of you, especially if he's still just a pup. But if he thinks this nasty shock had something to do with his stepping off the sidewalk, chances are he won't do it again, ever. This trainer has had that experience, anyway.

In all his years in working with dogs, no puppy treated in this fashion has ever needed a repeat lesson.

As for the older dog who's already a car chaser, your first job when he comes under your control is to break him of it. If you don't, you may soon lose your dog altogether. It helps to have the cooperation of a friend or assistant in this one. Have your helper drive the car slowly past while you ride alongside him. You must have the window open, so that you can throw a rock or set of rattling chains at the dog as soon as he gives chase. Don't let him see that you're the one who's throwing, but as soon as he starts nipping at the tires, let him have it. The object, as usual, is not to hurt the dog, but to scare him. You want him to associate something so unpleasant with car chasing that he'll give it up. It won't happen on the first trial, or the second. But eventually, given a lot of patience on your part, even this pernicious habit can be overcome.

No matter what vehicle your dog likes to chase, the same principle applies. Get a friend to ride a bike past your house and throw the chains out when the dog comes after him. You can do the same with friends who ride horses if that happens to be your special problem. Be sure to explain to your assistants that the idea isn't to punish the dog, but to scare him right out of his bad habits. They'll have to learn, just as you did, to deliver the deterrent in such a way that the dog doesn't realize what's being done. This is the only way to prevent him from bearing a grudge against people instead of blaming his own wrong actions. With all serious bad habits, it helps to tell your close friends what you're doing, and ask them to cooperate.

When the dog snaps at you, growls, or in any other way indicates threat, be firm. If you're trying to take an object out of his mouth, don't snatch your hand away, but hold on even tighter to the object, and give the command "Drop it!"

Most of the time, the dog will comply, somewhat amazed at your new assertiveness. When you give things to the dog, such as a bone or a dog biscuit, be sure he accepts them in the same civil way you want him to surrender objects. If he snaps at you when taking food from your hand, hang on, and tell him, "No." Just hang on to the bone—don't jerk it back from the dog; if you do that, he'll think you're teasing him, and he'll resent it deeply. Whenever he won't submit to what you want of him, be gentle, but firm. Don't give up. When you let your dog get the better of you by intimidation or nastiness, you're letting yourself in for a lot more of the same in the future.

A good general trick for discouraging bad habits is to distract the dog from whatever he's doing. Sometimes you can do this as easily as by just calling him to you, or by making a loud noise or cry that startles him. As soon as his attention is distracted from what you don't want, command him to do something you do want, such as "Come," and then praise him when he obeys. A very few dogs who really bite when they're handled will have to be muzzled. If the dog just snaps at you, without any real intention of hurting, you can get away with holding his mouth closed with your hand. It's amazing how helpless a dog or even a wolf is in this position, and he usually becomes docile right away. But if a muzzle is needed, don't be afraid to use one. A dog who bites his owners and trainers isn't a pet, he's a menace.

Even though un-learning is a lot harder than learning, dogs are versatile and adjustable. They're built to learn new things, in spite of the old saying, even when they're old. Proof of just how adaptable the dog is can be seen in his very domestic status. He was able to change, sometime in the distant past, from a wild, pack-roaming animal like the wolf to a human pet who shared the work and food of a species that was very different from his own. Individual dogs can change too, if the world around them changes. Your job as a trainer is to show the dog that things *have* changed. His old ways of doing things just don't work anymore, and he's going to have to try something new. If you succeed in actually convincing an animal of this change, his behavior will reverse itself at once. But it takes many trials for the lesson to sink in, even for human beings. Think how hard it is for older folks to get used to the changed customs of the young, for instance. If you remember your own devotion to certain bad habits, you'll be able to be more patient with your dog. And it's patience that will pay off in the long run.

Just how much can you expect a dog to learn? Given the right kind of training, patient and slow, there's very little most breeds can't learn to do. We've mentioned hunting dogs taught to bring back live baby ducklings in their mouths. Then there are the numerous stories of vicious cat chasers trained to curl up by the fire with the family feline, and the hungry pup who will wait uncomplainingly before a dish of food until he's commanded to eat. Most trainers think you can teach a dog almost anything if his disposition hasn't been ruined by cruelty, and if—big IF—you're willing to invest the necessary time and patience.

# IV
# FOR
# PUPPIES

*Puppies.*

*The author assumes* that the buyer of this book has already at least paper-trained the new puppy. If this is *not* the case, this bonus section is, of course, the start of any training program.

Although a puppy can't be fully housebroken until he's at least four months old, you can start right away letting him know what's expected in your house. Most people find that the easiest way to housebreak a pup is to paper-train him first, and wait until he's older to train him to go outside. A young puppy's immature bladder simply can't take the wait of four or five hours between walks.

Housebreaking starts the minute you bring the puppy home. Choose a small space, one that can be closed off, and cover the floor with newspapers. This is where your puppy should spend most of his time. You can make a bed for him out of rags or blankets in one corner. If he has come from a loving home, he'll already have been trained by his mother not to eliminate in the bed. Be sure that the rest of the area is *totally covered* with paper, so that the dog just can't go anywhere else. When he does use the papers, give him a pat on the head and a bit of praise. It won't do to make too much of it, or the dog will expect effusive praise every time he pees a drop or two. For the same reason, don't praise the puppy every single time he goes on the papers, or he'll come to expect that from you too. Sooner or later, you're bound to miss a time, and this will confuse the dog: he's done the marvelous deed, and he hasn't received his reward. The best expectation you can set up in him is that this behavior *usually* gets him reinforcement. That will be enough to get him to do it and keep doing it even if you're not there to pat his head each and every time.

Once the puppy picks out a favorite spot in the room for his toilet—and he will, don't worry—you can start to reduce the size of the paper-covered area. Take up most of the papers, but be sure you leave enough so that they're not easy for him to miss. He may change his mind about favorite spots, and if he does, move the papers there. After meals, and after he's been roughhousing, take him to the papers and praise him as usual when he performs. If the puppy spends time in any other room except his own, make sure there are papers there too. In not too long, he'll look around for the papers before he squats.

If all this makes it sound too easy, that's not our intent. As soon as you start trying to teach your puppy to do anything, you'll see why every dog trainer puts so much emphasis on patience. You must understand that every time you reward your dog, you only reinforce the behavior you praise. You don't ensure that he'll do the same thing every time, or that he'll never make any mistakes again. You simply increase the probability, by only a little bit, that he'll do what you want the next time. Each positive reinforcement increases the probability just a little bit more, but no one trial ever has a very big effect. Our kind of training, which concentrates exclusively on positive reinforcement, doesn't bring the dramatic, one-trial results of some of the more negative methods. But the negative methods can and usually do have long-term negative effects on the personality and behavior of the dog. Swatting or shouting at the puppy will make him behave in order to avoid your wrath. Fear may make a noticeable, even a remarkable, change in him. But your negative control may also teach him to hate and fear *you*. He'll do things not to win your love and get closer to you, but just to avoid punishment. He may even turn sneaky and mean. And once these characteristics are induced in an animal, they're next to impossible to stamp out.

For this reason, we say emphatically, don't punish the dog when he messes! If you see your puppy start to go in the wrong spot, quickly pick him up and put him on the papers. Then praise him, as usual, for going where he's supposed to. If you're too far away to reach the puppy, don't go racing toward him and swoop him up like a threatening chicken hawk. This will scare him as much as, if not more than, a spanking. Instead, try whistling or calling to him, just to distract his attention. Then, if he stops what he's doing, go over, pick him up, and put him on those ever-present papers. Praise him then, even if he doesn't go. The reward is partly for his having ceased to do what you didn't want.

There are many methods of switching from paper training to real housebreaking, including putting down smaller and smaller areas of paper, or gradually sliding the paper out under the back door so that the dog will scratch to go out. We think the best way is simply to replace the old learning with new. This means that when the dog has sufficient muscular control—usually at about four or five months—you should pick up all papers. Now, of course, he must be taken outside several times a day to relieve himself. If you have an enclosed backyard, the easiest thing to do is give the puppy the run of the yard. Whenever he messes in the house, or even looks as though he's about to, scoot him out the back door. Don't forget the reinforcement when he does eliminate in the yard. During this sometimes trying period, there's only one thing you must endeavor not to do: lose your temper. Be prepared for the zigzag course of the dog's learning. Just when you think he really has got it down perfectly, that's when he'll make another mistake. You'll feel exasperation, and there's nothing wrong with feeling it. But be careful about expressing it to the dog. He'll feel disapproval as a punishment, and react accordingly. As much as you can, confine your expressions to approval of good behavior, rather than disapproval of bad.

If you live in the city, or just don't have a fenced yard for your pet, he'll have to be leash-trained before he can be properly housebroken. The best way to do this is to get the pup used to wearing a collar right away. When he's completely at ease with the collar, try attaching a leash to it for a few minutes around the house. You can lead him, or just let him drag it after him as he wanders about. If you do this from the time you bring the puppy home, he'll be completely familiar with the leash before he's old enough to be taken outside to eliminate.

When you do take him out, make the first walks purely for pleasure. Never tug at the dog on the street, especially not when he's first using the leash. Let him lead you wherever he wants to go. These pleasure walks should begin well before you start taking the dog out with expectations of housebreaking. Very soon, the pup will start to associate the leash with excitement and pleasure. He'll like nothing better than walking with you. Then, when he's eager to have the leash snapped on, you can begin to take him for walks that mean business.

The importance of leash training is often ignored by people who live in suburban areas, and sometimes even by city-dwelling pet owners. But leash laws are becoming stricter, and more strictly enforced, all the time. We dog lovers have to learn to live and let live our fellow citizens, some of whom are so mistaken as to actually dislike pets. For the sake of our dogs and of our fellow citizens, all of us who keep animals should observe the laws that concern them. Teach your pup to enjoy his walks on the leash, and he'll never miss the wandering that only country dogs can be permitted. Whenever you can, take him to the beach or the woods or the park for a real run off the leash. But on the streets, even in the suburbs, the leash is a must.

If your pup balks when you're walking him, bend over and pat your knee, calling him to you with whatever command you normally use. Or lean down and pat the sidewalk to attract his attention. Give him reinforcement when he comes to you, but never punish him when he doesn't. If necessary, give the leash a sharp jerk, purely to startle the pup into action. Immediately let the line go slack, and praise the dog for walking toward you, even if it's only one step. Never drag the dog along the street by the neck. No matter how long it takes—and it really won't take as long as you anticipate when you're impatient—coax the pup rather than forcing him. If you're in a rush, don't choose that time to walk the dog. Remember that if you're really too busy to train your dog, you probably shouldn't get one at all. Owning a pet is a real commitment for people, especially since hardly any of us live on farms where the animal can safely and conveniently have the run of the place.

When the pup is completely at home with the collar and leash, you can start real housebreaking. By this time, the dog is from four to six months old, and he has enough control to wait for his walks before eliminating. All the papers have been taken up, and you're ready to start. During the housebreaking period, which is a time of intensive work for both you and the dog, you must never let the puppy have free run of the house. Whenever you are away or sleeping, confine the animal to a very small space—smaller than the puppy space he has been living in with his newspapers. This makes use of the first lesson he learned from his mother— not to foul his immediate surroundings. He has a strong aversion to soiling the place where he sleeps.

Your housebreaking chore will be much easier if you don't let the dog make mistakes. This means that you really have to watch him every minute, or else confine him. Sometimes, the only way to keep him in a really small space is to tie him by his leash to the radiator or a table leg. This is inconvenient for both of you, but not cruel. Remember, the more vigilant you are now, the shorter the housebreaking period will be. There will be accidents, though, no matter how closely you keep watch. If you see the dog start to urinate or defecate, try the trick of distracting him, then praising him if he stops. Immediately take him outside so that he can do his duty in the proper place. But if he succeeds in going in the house, it will be enough to indicate your displeasure by tone of voice. Say, "Bad dog!" and let it go at that. The important part of our training method is positive reinforcement, not negative. Above all, don't slap the puppy around or rub his nose in his messes. That only teaches him hate and fear.

In any training, but especially in a matter as urgent as housebreaking, regularity and consistency are vital. The dog should eat at regular intervals, and he should be let out or walked immediately after eating. The last feeding, if you expect the pup to stay dry during the night, should be no later than six in the evening, and should consist mostly of solids. Be sure you take him out right after dinner, and again before bedtime. In this way, the dog will soon learn exactly what to expect, and what is expected of him. This makes the job much easier for both of you. One word of caution: It is unwise to be a perfectionist about this or any other aspect of dog training. There will always be lapses and mistakes. Sometimes a dog, even a grown-up and well-trained one, will insist on peeing when he's left in the house alone, for example, or when someone in the family has offended him in some other way. When this happens, it is a fight between you (or whoever has offended him) and the dog. If you react with violence or rage, it constitutes a victory for the dog. He has succeeded in making you pay attention to him. The best way to discourage such attempts to get your goat is to ignore them as much as possible, except for trying to distract the dog if you catch him in the act. If these acts on the part of a fully trained, adult dog fail to get a rise out of you, he'll leave off after a while. In a puppy, however, it serves some purpose to actively express your disapproval.

The first months of any new puppy are spent learning rudimentary good manners. Of these, housebreaking is probably the most important. Nevertheless, there are lots and lots of other little things the pup learns before he ever gets to basic obedience training. He learns about his masters: what makes them happy or unhappy, and how to tell which they are by tone of voice and bodily attitude. He learns his name, and lots of other words like "come," "no," "outside," "car," "dinner," and whichever others you use consistently to him. He learns to play with the family in the way that pleases them. And he learns, through the methods discussed in the last section, to forgo bad habits like chewing on valuables or howling during the night.

Most of all, your puppy is a new member of your family. In order for your association to be long and happy, he has to learn to love and trust his human friends. Time spent loving and playing with your pup will be paid back in faithfulness all the years he lives with you. Treat him well, cuddle and love him, and you will make your job as an obedience trainer infinitely easier. And you'll be making sure that you achieve the pleasure and companionship you were seeking when you chose to get a puppy in the first place. For both you and the puppy, the password is "Enjoy."

# INDEX